MW01469027

"I am your Jesus, born Incarnate. I have come to speak to you about the virtue of love. Holy Love is, as you know, the two great commandments: love God above all else and your neighbor as yourself. It is the embrace of all Ten Commandments. Holy Love is the Immaculate Heart of My Mother. It is the Divine Will of God."

"Holy Love can be likened to the sun, which spills its rays over the earth enlightening the shadows of darkness. It is like the keys to the kingdom I entrusted to My apostle Peter. It is the door to My Sacred Heart and union with Divine Love."

"Holy Love is the harmony between man, nature, and the Creator. It is the interpretation of the law and the means of all sanctification."

"The will of man must choose Holy Love. It is not open to debate, and stands undaunted in the face of discernment. Holy Love cannot be judged, for it is the judge."

"Holy Love is offered in every present moment and follows the soul into eternity."

"You will make this known."

SELF-LOVE   vs.   HOLY LOVE

"Is motivated towards self-advantage in thought, word and deed."	"Is motivated in every thought, word, and action by love of God and neighbor as self."
"Sees only others' faults, not his own. Considers himself on the right path—perhaps even humble and virtuous."	"Sees himself full of imperfections. Is always seeking to be perfected through love. Considers everyone more humble and holy than himself."
"Holds a checklist in his heart of every wrong perpetrated against him."	"Imitates Divine Mercy as best he can. Is compassionate and forgiving."
"Is quick to anger and stands vigil over his own rights making certain they are not transgressed."	"Is patient. Takes notes of others' needs and concerns."
"Hangs on to his own opinions refusing to surrender to another viewpoint."	"Offers his own opinions but listens to others and lends them equal merit with his own."
"Takes pride in his own achievements. May even take pride in his spiritual progress."	"Realizes all things proceed from God; that without God he is capable of no good thing. All good comes from grace."

SELF-LOVE vs. HOLY LOVE

"Sees himself and the world as the be-all/end-all. His only pleasure is thus achieved though the world."	"Takes joy in storing up heavenly treasure; in growing closer to God and deeper in holiness. Knows the difference between earthly pleasures and spiritual joy."
"Uses the goods of the world to satisfy self."	"Uses the goods of the world to satisfy quest for holiness."
"Objects to every cross. Sees trials as a curse. Resents others' good fortune."	"Surrenders to the cross through love as Jesus did. Sees crosses as a grace to be used to convert others."
"Prays only for himself and his own needs."	"Prays for all in need."
"Cannot accept God's Will. Becomes bitter over trials."	"Accepts God's Will with a loving heart even when difficult."

(Given to Maureen Sweeney-Kyle by Blessed Mother on August 18, 1997)

"Tonight I have come to ask that all of My brothers and sisters unite in prayer towards their own personal holiness. Do not let Satan discourage you in this… He would have you think you have prayed enough, you have sacrificed enough. It is never too much. I am with you in your efforts towards holiness."

Jesus
February 29, 2008

United Hearts Book

of

Prayers and Meditations

Prayers from Heaven
for Missionary Servants of Holy Love
January 2001 – April 2008

These prayers are offered for private meditation. Unless otherwise indicated, they were given to the Visionary, Maureen Sweeney-Kyle, MSHL.

Archangel Gabriel Enterprises Inc.

This volume contains the prayers and meditations given by Heaven from January of 2001 through April of 2008. Please see the *Triumphant Hearts Prayer Book* for the prayers and meditations received through December of 2000. All messages and prayers from Heaven are posted on our website at:

http://www.holylove.org.

Current Canonical Explanation:
Response to Apparitions and Visionaries
for Roman Catholics

Since the abolition of Canon 1399 and 2318 of the former Code of Canon Law by Paul VI in AAS58 (1966) page 1186, publications about new apparitions, revelation, prophecies, miracles, etc., have been allowed to be distributed and read by the faithful without the express permission of the Church, providing that they contain nothing which contravenes faith and morals. This means, no imprimatur is necessary.

The Discernment of Visionaries
and Apparitions Today

by Albert J. Hebert, S.M., Page III

Published by:
©2008 Archangel Gabriel Enterprises Inc.
North Ridgeville, OH 44039   All rights reserved
ISBN: 978-1-937800-37-6

Dedicated To

The United Hearts Of

The Holy Trinity And

Immaculate Mary

"Freely you have received, freely give." (Mt. 10:8)
This book is a gift to you. We believe the messages are from God. If they touch your heart buy a copy for a friend. Jesus desires that we "Make this known". For a paperback, free digital copy, or to receive free daily messages see :**www.holylove.org**. Enter the **Chambers of the United Hearts** with free day calendar: **www.unitedheartsdaycalendar.com**

CONTENTS

* *

PART ONE – SANCTIFY THE DAY

PART TWO – PRAYERS AND DEVOTIONS

PART THREE – PRAYERS FOR THE LIVING AND THE DEAD

PART FOUR – THE BATTLE FOR TRUTH

ABOUT THE APPARITIONS

❅❅

Since 1985, Jesus and Blessed Mother have been appearing to Maureen Sweeney-Kyle on an almost daily basis and have given her a series of missions to accomplish.

1986–1990
OUR LADY, PROTECTRESS OF THE FAITH

NOTE: On August 28, 1988, Our Lady came as "Guardian of the Faith" to Visionary, Patricia Talbot, of Cuenca, Ecuador, in South America. In 1991, the Bishops of Ibarra and Guayaquil in Ecuador approved the movement which contains the name "Guardian of the Faith" and thus implicitly the title.

1990–1993
PROJECT MERCY
(Nationwide Anti-Abortion Rosary Crusades)

1993–Present
The combined Revelations of **MARY, REFUGE OF HOLY LOVE** and the **CHAMBERS OF THE UNITED HEARTS**. In 1993, Our Lady asked that this Mission be known as **HOLY LOVE MINISTRIES**.

Visionary:

Maureen Sweeney-Kyle is a very shy, timid and frail housewife and grandmother. She grew up and still resides in the Cleveland, Ohio area with her husband. In 1993, Our Lady began **Holy Love Ministries** and then requested that the Ministry procure property for a shrine in Lorain County, Ohio. This was accomplished in 1995. This 115-acre shrine is now known as **Maranatha Spring and Shrine**, the home of **Holy Love Ministries**, an Ecumenical Lay Apostolate to make known to the world the Chambers of the United Hearts.

Spiritual Director:

Over the past twenty years, Maureen has had four spiritual directors who have been experts in Marian Theology.

On the joyful occasion of the visit by the visionary, Maureen Sweeney-Kyle, with Pope John Paul II in August of 1999. Her husband, Don (*lower right*), Archbishop Gabriel Ganaka (*top left*), and Rev. Frank Kenney, her Spiritual Director (1994-2004) (*top center*), accompanied her on the visit.

ABOUT THE COMPLETE IMAGE OF THE UNITED HEARTS OF THE HOLY TRINITY AND IMMACULATE MARY
(Front Cover)

* *

January 18, 2007

As I (Maureen) was praying in my prayer room, a large Flame appeared. Then I heard a voice that said:

"All praise be the Blessed Trinity. I am God the Father."

"You see My Heart before you as a massive Flame. It is the Flame of My Eternal, Divine Will which burns before you. It is this Flame that is the embodiment of Perfect Love and My Divine Will. My Heart is a Flame which engulfs the United Hearts of Jesus and Mary—of Holy and Divine Love—melting Them into Divine Union with My Will, never to be separated."

"So you see, I present to you a new Image—the complete Image of Love—the Union of Holy and Divine Love completely immersed in the Flame of My Fatherly Heart, which is the Divine Will. Remembering that My Will is made up of Divine Love and Divine Mercy, you must see My Heart as the Will of Mercy and Love. It is the perfection I invite all people and all nations to step into, beginning with the Heart of Mary. It is Eternally My Will in you."

February 17, 2007

St. Thomas Aquinas says: "Praise be to Jesus."

"The Light which surrounds the Image of the United Hearts is the Light of the Holy Spirit, which inspires the soul to enter into a relationship with Holy and Divine Love. It is the Holy Spirit that leads the soul through the process of purification and challenges the heart to go deeper and ever deeper into Divine Love."

"So you see the completeness of this Revelation of the United Hearts."

June 2, 2007

I see the Heart of the Father as a huge Flame. He says: "I am the Eternal Now."

"I have come to enlighten the heart of the world as to the significance of the new Image of the United Hearts of the Holy Trinity and Immaculate Mary."

"In the world, there is one Marian dogma yet to be proclaimed; that of, *Mary, Mediatrix, Co-Redemptrix and Advocate.* In this new Image, this dogma is readily evident, for Mary's Heart is immersed in the Heart of Her Son and surrounded by Her Spouse, the Holy Spirit. Further, the United Hearts of Jesus and Mary are both immersed in the Flame of the Eternal Now—My Paternal Heart."

"The Immaculate Heart is the Gateway to the New Jerusalem—the portal to the Divine Will—through which the Holy Trinity pours all grace into the world.

United to the Sacred Heart of Her Son, Mary suffered in Her own Heart, every wound and insult of the Passion with greater intensity than any human. She is closer to the Holy Trinity than any mortal ever was or will be. Therefore, She is a most powerful Advocate."

"Present the doctrine of this new Image to the world."

June 5, 2007
Monthly Message to All People and Every Nation

Jesus and Blessed Mother are here. Their Hearts are exposed. Blessed Mother says: "Praise be to Jesus." Jesus says: "I am your Jesus, born Incarnate."

Jesus: "I have come to help the world understand these times in which you live. The advent of the Image of the United Hearts of the Holy Trinity and Immaculate Mary marks an importance you do not readily realize. The introduction of this Image into the world opens the Book of Revelation as regards to events in the world at large. Watch and listen as the pages turn, for I tell you, the Image presented to you is apocalyptic in its entirety."

"During this age of advanced technologies, people of all nations are rubbing shoulders through communications and faster travel. It is an age when, as never before, the boundaries of countries and ideologies are challenged. I come to you hoping to spread love amongst all people and all nations. Others, influenced by Satan, promote hatred. This is the battle between good and evil that the Adversary has engaged you in. While it used to be confined to certain areas or specific people in the world, or hidden in hearts, now it has spread to every nation. Satan uses modern technology to fan the flames of his war of deceit."

"I do not use symbols to speak to you now. I tell you in straightforward language these truths. The righteous who slip from the path of good will bring more to bear upon this generation than the ones who never knew Me. Those who call Me their Lord and Master through pretense, but are devoted to self alone, will be visited by justice. Those who say they love Me, but do not trust Me, have fallen victim to Satan's lies and will have their trust continually tested. Love and trust go hand in hand."

"What lies in the future calls you to remain close to Me, for I am The Way, The Truth and The Life. Security by any other means is false."

"I do not come to you seeking approvals. I come seeking souls. As children of the light, I invoke you, pray that your numbers increase. In this way, the Remnant Faithful will be strengthened. Each one of you is called to apostleship, to be a disciple of Holy and Divine Love. The Woman clothed with the sun is waiting to call all people and all nations into the purification of the United Hearts. Do not resist Her."

"I know all the petitions in hearts here today. Some will receive what they desire; others will receive God's Will for them, but will not be satisfied."

"Today I ask you, My brothers and sisters, to allow My Victory to come into your hearts. Allow Me to build up the Kingdom of the Divine Will within your hearts in this present moment. To do so is to live always in the truth that is Holy and Divine Love."

"My brothers and sisters, We're blessing you with the Blessing of Our United Hearts."

ABOUT PRAYER, FASTING AND SACRIFICE

* *

"My brothers and sisters, tonight I invite you to understand that your smallest effort in prayer, sacrifice or fasting does not remain small but affects the entire cosmos—the whole universe; therefore, do not be discouraged in the least little effort, for I take it and make it great."

Jesus
April 30, 2007

PRAYER LIFE

Jesus is here with His Heart exposed. He says: "I am your Jesus, born Incarnate."

"My brothers and sisters, once again I have come to encourage you in your prayer lives. Every prayer counts—every prayer is heard and opens the door of communication between Heaven and earth. Just as on earth, sometimes doors are open only a crack—it is true with prayers as well. The more love you have in your heart when you pray, the wider the door of communication opens."

"Tonight I'm blessing you with My Blessing of Divine Love."

(January 27, 2006)

St. Thomas Aquinas comes. He says: "Praise be to Jesus."

"I have come to encourage all those who seek holiness. If your spirit is comprised of all the virtues you embrace, please understand that your prayer life is the mortar that holds the bricks of virtue in place. Without mortar, bricks crumble and fall. Without prayers, virtues are replaced with weaknesses and sin. A solid brick wall is impregnable by fire. A brick wall without mortar can be easily toppled, and profaned by Satan's flames of deceit."

"When you neglect your everyday prayer life, you leave room for Satan to enter your heart with his suggestions. Then you fall into self-pity, egoism, avarice and more. What's more, you are not in harmony with God's Divine Will and, therefore, you do not see this happening. Your spirit becomes synchronized with Satan's agenda instead of God's Will which is a life of virtue. It is then you become the adversary's tool, which he uses to reach others."

"Understand, then, the impact your prayer life has—not only on yourself—but others, as well. If you do not pray, the motives of your thoughts, words and deeds are easily taken over by self-love."

"I tell you these things to make you stronger in Holy and Divine Love, and thus to strengthen the Mission."

(January 7, 2006)

To Priests And Lay People

St. John Vianney: "I have come to tell each one of you that anything you do without love in your heart is wasted. Priests in particular must pray for love of prayer, sacrifice and penance, for this is the way of conversion for their flock that they have been entrusted with. Do not hesitate to ask me to intercede for you, whether you are a priest or lay person. This is a special grace to love penance, prayer and sacrifice. I will help you with it."

(July 14, 2006)

WHEN YOU PRAY

1. Begin with the Sign of the Cross

THE SIGN OF THE CROSS

*I*n the Name of the Father, and of the Son, and of the Holy Spirit. Amen.

Our Lady: "Dear Children, I am asking you to remember that the Sign of the Cross is a prayer. It is not just words to be rushed through to get to the real prayers. When said devoutly, from the heart, it is an efficacious prayer in preparation for all prayers to follow."

2. Hold a Crucifix in your hands

Jesus: "Have a clear understanding of My Passion. When you pray, pray with a crucifix in your hands."
(March 28, 2003)

3. Join your prayers to every prayer ever prayed throughout time

Jesus: "When you pray, join your prayers to every prayer that was ever prayed and every prayer that ever will be prayed so that My Father will be greatly honored by every syllable."
(January 25, 2005)

4. Unite your prayers to the Hearts of Jesus and Mary

Jesus: "How often souls depend on your prayers. Unite them to the Hearts of Jesus and Mary."
(March 31, 1996)

5. Cover your prayers with the Most Precious Blood

Our Lady: "My dear, dear children, when you pray, cover your prayers with the Most Precious Blood of My Beloved Son, Jesus."
(June 19, 2003)

6. Pray with a heart full of love for Jesus and Mary

Jesus: "Do not pray out of duty, but pray because you love Me; because you love My Mother, and you desire to please Us. This is the way to make your prayers more powerful."

(March 6, 2006)

7. Strengthen prayer with sacrifice

Our Lady: "When sacrifice is added to prayers, it is twice as strong."

(June 8, 1998)

St. Thomas Aquinas: "I invite you to contemplate this for a moment. A skillful chef uses only the best ingredients for his dishes. A skillful carpenter chooses the best wood and uses the best tools when he creates a piece of furniture. When a soul prays or sacrifices, he is, in fact, creating a gift to give to Jesus or to Jesus through Mary. Like the skillful artisans in the world, he should choose the best implements and finest materials."

"In prayer and sacrifice, the ingredient most important—the tool which lends most power and effectiveness—is Holy Love in the heart. Next to this should be Holy Humility, which combined with Holy Love, allows the soul to surrender completely to the Divine Will of the Father. The stronger these two are in the soul during prayer and sacrifice, the more effective the petitions of the heart."

"In Christ's Agony in the Garden, you can plainly see these two—love and humility—at work. Once Jesus resolved to accept His suffering, He never looked back. He allowed Himself to be stripped of everything at the Tenth Station out of love and humility."

"Consider, now, the crosses in your own life, and pray to increase in love and humility. This way, you will surrender more completely to God's Divine Will, and your prayers and sacrifices will be more worthy."

(March 14, 2006)

8. Pray often and from the heart

Jesus: "My brothers and sisters, tonight realize that your prayers offered with humility and heartfelt love ransom many souls from the path of perdition and onto the path of righteousness. Persevere, then, in heartfelt prayer, for many souls depend on your efforts. Do not be discouraged in any way, for this is Satan trying to dissuade you from the path of righteousness."

(June 1, 2007)

Jesus: "The present moments that are wasted cause My Arm of Justice to weigh heavy. It is only My Mother's prayers and your prayers, as well, that are holding it back—keeping it from falling. Tonight, I tell you, you must not give up praying. Pray often and from the heart so that we can win this battle—good against evil."

(August 18, 2006)

WHEN YOU FAST

1. Fast from sin

Our Lady of Grace: "Dear children, I desire much more than your fasts from food that you enjoy. I desire that you fast from any sin. In this way you will make recompense to the sorrowing and grieving Heart of My Beloved Son."

(July 11, 1996)

2. Fast from your own will/self-love

Mary, Refuge of Holy Love: "While it is very good and acceptable to fast on bread and water, it is not good to try this if you are ill or if such a fast would threaten your health. The best fast is to fast from your own will. Your will is self-love. I have given you these guidelines. Surrender being in the spotlight, having your own way, doing as you choose when you choose it. Make yourself little."

(October 5, 1997)

23

WHEN YOU SACRIFICE

1. Lose sight of yourself and focus on Jesus

St. Thomas Aquinas: "Dear child, I have come to help you understand how to make purer sacrifices. Take, for instance, the multitude of buttons down the front of my cassock—quite the challenge for one so portly as your Thomas."

"When I undertook the fastening of those buttons, I surrendered all thought of cost to me and focused on Jesus. With each button I pictured myself kissing the Wounds of Jesus—wiping His Bloodied Face and consoling His Sorrowful Mother."

"This is how to give everything to the Lord. Lose sight of yourself and focus on Him."

(May 2, 2005)

2. Let every sacrifice be a sacrifice of love

Jesus: "I ask you to let every sacrifice be a sacrifice of love. Do not make sacrifices with much regret but with love, and they will be more worthwhile. They will strengthen you spiritually; then I will grant you what you ask in prayer."

(March 13, 2006)

Jesus: "Today I tell you, it is sacrificial love that wins the conversion of souls. When you sacrifice with a loving heart for the good of another, I am able to reach out with strength and power which you have earned for that soul through sacrificial love."

"Love must be at the heart of all prayer, all good works, all sacrifice; the deeper the love, the more meritorious the action. I desire all people realize this so as to strengthen My army against evil."

(October 11, 2007)

St. Therese of the Child Jesus: "Today you have a snowstorm outside. If only one flake fell, it would not amount to much. It is many flakes together that form the great snowdrifts. It is the way with sacrifices, as well. Many little, humble sacrifices amount to much in God's Eyes. Never allow Satan to convince you otherwise. Each sacrifice is as valuable as the depth of Holy Love in the heart when it is offered. That is what God looks at—not the cost of the sacrifice to the soul."

(December 16, 2007)

3. Recipe for a good sacrifice

St. Therese of the Child Jesus: "Write down what I have come to tell you, child. This is the recipe for a good sacrifice."

"First and foremost, the sacrifice should arise from a heart full of love. Otherwise, what is surrendered to God is given half-heartedly. The sacrifice is only as worthy as the depth of love with which it is offered. To put it another way, if the sacrifice

25

were a delicious morsel of food, it would only be as good as the ingredients used to prepare it."

"Any sacrifice done impatiently, angrily or with little Holy Love, merits the soul little consolation in this life, reward in the next life, and perhaps even a longer stay in Purgatory."

"Always serve God and neighbor as a little child whose sole purpose is to please his parents out of love."

(October 1, 2005)

4. Offer the greatest and most perfect sacrifice—to live in Holy Love in every present moment

Jesus: "Do not wonder what type of sacrifice to offer Me; for the greatest and most perfect of all sacrifices is to live in Holy Love in every present moment. To do so dictates a total dying to self. This is the sum total of all I ask."

(February 9, 2008)

SATAN'S TACTICS

"I am your Jesus, born Incarnate. I have come to help you recognize Satan's tactics so that you will not be under his influence. Satan is in confusion, anger and fear. He is the carrier of lack of peace. He tries to discourage any positive effort by telling you there is no way out of certain situations, that prayer and sacrifice are useless because the petitions in your heart are too awesome for any prayer to be effective."

"If none of this works and you persevere in prayer, he moves to a higher level. He tells you that which you are praying for is probably not the Divine Will of God; therefore, better to give it up, for if you got what you prayed for it would be disastrous anyway. If you still do not give up, he brings in one distraction after another as you pray, hoping to keep you from prayer altogether."

"He is untiring in his efforts. He puts people in your life that upset you. Some are his cohorts—others unwittingly his puppets. Each soul must be aware of these insidious tactics of the enemy in order not to succumb to them."

"You will please make this known."

(March 11, 2004)

St. John Vianney: "My brothers and sisters, if you do not recognize the portal that Satan comes through to reach the inner recesses of your heart with his temptations—if you do not recognize the path he draws you upon with his evil inspirations—then you are giving him free reign in your hearts and in your lives. This is especially true of priests who are the most popular targets of evil. You must pray for the wisdom to recognize and to know the enemy; then you will be ready for his next attack, and he will not trip you up."

(August 11, 2006)

Ask Your Guardian Angel For Help

Jesus: "I have come to remind you to let Holy Love stand vigil over your heart in every present moment. Ask your Guardian Angel for his help in this regard. Otherwise the enemy will find the same port of entry into your thoughts, your actions and your decisions. You must be cognizant of the way that Satan operates if you intend to oppose him."

(July 28, 2006)

PART ONE

Sanctify The Day

Chapter 1. *Morning Prayers*

* *

In This Chapter:

* *

"If you desire to love Me more and go deeper into the Chambers of Our United Hearts, then sanctify your daily routine with prayer and offer everything with a loving heart."

Jesus
Monthly Message to
All People and Every Nation
May 5, 2004

PRAYERS UPON ARISING

VICTIMHOOD OF LOVE PRAYER

Dear Jesus, in this present moment, for love of You, I accept the cross no matter what form it takes. I desire to heal Your wounded Heart through this Victimhood of Love. Amen.

"Each day and in every present moment, the cross takes on a new form in every person's life. Be ready by accepting the cross for love of Me. This is the way of Divine Victimhood—the way to become a Victim of Love. In your acceptance is your surrender. When you arise, pray thus...Repeat this prayer throughout the day or whenever the cross presents itself in a difficult way."

Jesus
August 31, 2006

PRAYER FOR PERSONAL SANCTIFICATION IN THE PRESENT MOMENT

*H*eavenly Father, I desire to live in your Divine Will in every present moment by living in Holy Love in thought, word and deed.

When I am distracted or tempted, I ask my guardian angel to remind me of the present moment so that I may sanctify each moment through Holy Love. Amen.

"I desire your complete submission to My Father's Will in every present moment. Therefore, begin each day with this prayer."

Jesus
July 30, 2005

Ask The Holy Angels To Flood Your Heart With Holy Love

St. Thomas Aquinas: "Ask the holy angels to keep you on course. **When you arise in the morning, ask the angels to flood your heart with love of God and neighbor**. Do not underestimate the power of this practice. The Triune God desires that you have every advantage to lead you towards sanctity."

(December 16, 2005)

PRAYER TO BE VIRTUOUS TODAY

*D*ear Jesus, through the Immaculate Heart of Mary, open my heart to the grace I need to be perfected in virtue today in every present moment. Amen.

"The soul must never consider himself perfect in any virtue. He should never think: 'I was patient yesterday so now I have perfected the virtue of patience'—for the next test may be even greater than the last. Each soul needs to ask for the grace upon arising to be virtuous throughout the day."

Jesus
March 10, 2003

CONSECRATION TO SELF-DENIAL

"This is the way to live every day, giving God the glory when you arise. With all your heart, say:"

*D*ear Jesus, Divine and Beloved Savior, today I surrender to You every pain—physical, spiritual or emotional. I will not complain about inconveniences, demands upon my time, breaches of privacy or the rudeness of those You put in my life today. With Your help, I will accept each present moment with Holy Love. Amen.

"This is the loving, sweet surrender of your whole life, beginning with the present moment. This little prayer is the consecration to self-denial. Recite it with love."

"....if you recite it in the morning, then great and small sacrifices that you may forget to offer the Lord have already been given to Him."

St. Martin de Porres
November 3, 2006

MORNING SURRENDER PRAYER

*H*elp me, my Jesus. Help me to give You my whole heart just as You gave Yourself entirely to me in Your Passion and Death—just as You give Yourself completely to me in every Mass and in the Holy Eucharist.

Stand guard over my senses so that my heart will not be conflicted by things of the world or others' opinions.

In this present moment, assist me in giving to You an undivided heart.

"Say this prayer from the heart every morning. I am listening."

Jesus
October 22, 2007

Surrender Everything As You Arise And When You Retire

Jesus: "My brothers and sisters, just as We have been your safe harbor during this storm [there were heavy winds and rain], learn to **surrender everything to My provision and My Mother's protection** during every difficulty of life. Learn to do this as you retire at night, and once again when you arise in the morning."

(July 29, 2002)

DAILY OFFERINGS

CONSECRATION TO THE DIVINE WILL

*H*eavenly Father, I desire that You place the Seal of Your Divine Will upon my heart. Thus, I will accept Your Will in all situations and in every present moment. I will accept all things as from Your Hand for the good of my salvation and the salvation of others. Amen.

Two Angels adoring Jesus at Adoration
October 15, 2001

PRAYER OF SURRENDER TO HOLY AND DIVINE LOVE

*D*ear United Hearts of Jesus and Mary, I desire to surrender to Holy and Divine Love in all things, in all ways and in every present moment. Send me the grace so that I may do this. Help me as I try to respond to this grace. Be my protection and provision. Take up Your Reign in my heart. Amen.

Jesus
The Revelation of Our United Hearts
February 1, 2001

CONSECRATION TO HOLY LOVE IN THE PRESENT MOMENT

*H*eavenly Father, I consecrate my heart in this present moment to Holy Love. Keep me mindful of this throughout the day so that all my thoughts and actions will proceed from Holy Love."

I cover this petition with the Most Precious Blood of Jesus, your Son, and surround it with the Tears of His Most Sorrowful Mother. Amen.

"Jesus desires that you consecrate your day to Holy Love."

St. Thomas Aquinas
January 21, 2002

PRAYER FOR SPIRITUAL LITTLENESS

Dear Jesus, I wish to come to you as a little child. As a child, I desire only to appeal to you. In this effort, I reject the pomp of the world. I embrace the truth of humility which reveals to me where I am in God's Eyes. I seek only God's approval in every present moment.

Thus I surrender my own will and my human nature to the Divine Will of God. In doing so, I do not chase after pleasures or importance in human eyes. I allow God complete mastery over my heart, trusting always in His plans for me. Amen.

Jesus
November 15, 2004

Have The Heart Of A Child

Mary, Refuge of Holy Love: "Have the heart of a little child which holds no guile or self-interest, but only love. I am the Patroness of the spiritual child that comes to Me in littleness."

(June 24, 2006)

PRAYER OF SUBMISSION TO DIVINE LOVE

Dear Jesus, pin my heart next to Your Most Sacred Heart on the Cross. Help me to die to the world as You did. Make my heart impervious to the arrows of slander and false accusations.

Collect my heart and all its emotions and immerse it in the Flame of Divine Love—the Flame of Your Heart. There, protect me from the allurements of the world. Preserve in my heart all that is pleasing to You, and strike far from it any seduction of Satan. Amen.

Ezra, Angel of Mercy and Love—
The One Who Protects the Mission
October 16, 2002

PRAYER OF CONSECRATION TO THE TRUTH

Your words, Lord, are Light and Truth. Your Provision, Your Mercy and Your Love come to me clothed in truth.

Help me always to live in Your Truth. Assist me in recognizing Satan's deceit in my own thoughts and in the thoughts, words and actions of others. Do not let humility elude me, as I know humility is truth itself. Amen.

Jesus
July 13, 2007

PRAYER TO THE PRECIOUS BLOOD

Sweet Precious Blood of Jesus, pour out upon this Mission and the Confraternity. Set us free from anything that may distract our journey into the United Hearts. Immerse us in Divine Love—Divine Mercy. Amen.

Jesus
February 17, 2004

PRECIOUS BLOOD DEVOTION

"I am your Jesus, born Incarnate, risen from the dead. Alleluia!"

"I offer, through you, this devotion to the world of the sacrifice of My Most Precious Blood. The devotion is short, but powerful; it is five 'Hail Marys."

"These are the meditations:"

1. "The sacrifice of the shedding of My Blood under the whips and thorns perpetrated by My persecutors;" *Hail Mary…*

2. "The sacrifice of the shedding of My Blood as I was nailed to the Cross;" *Hail Mary…*

3. "The sacrifice of the shedding of My Blood as My Heart was pierced by the sword;" *Hail Mary…*

4.   "The sacrifice of the shedding of My Blood in every Mass;" *Hail Mary…*

5.   "The sacrifice of the shedding of My Blood as I abide Body, Blood, Soul and Divinity in the tabernacles of the world." *Hail Mary…*

April 11, 2004
Easter Sunday

Promises

"I am your Jesus, born Incarnate raised from the dead. Alleluia!"

"I am prepared to relay to you My promises to those who recite the five 'Hail Marys' venerating the shedding of My Most Precious Blood."

1.   "First and foremost, this is a prompt and certain protection from Satan's attacks."

2.   "Secondly, this veneration will uncover Satan's attacks where they lay hidden."

3.   "Thirdly, it is a tool on the path of perfection within the soul, taking it deeper into the Chambers of Our United Hearts."

"You will make this known."

April 12, 2004

PRAYER FOR DEEPER HOLINESS THROUGH HUMILITY AND LOVE

*H*eavenly Father, I petition Your Paternal Heart in this present moment to carry my heart deeper into Holy Love and Holy Humility. I realize that my free will must cooperate with Your Divine Will so that humility and love can increase in me.

I give You my will now, fully accepting whatever it may please You to send me, as I choose to be a little martyr of love in Your Hands. Amen.

"I have come to help you understand that your holiness and sanctification will only reach the depth of the humility and love in your heart. Therefore, in order to deepen your journey into the Chambers of the United Hearts, each one should pray daily for deeper love and humility, for on these two every virtue has its foundation."

St. Thomas Aquinas
April 17, 2006

MISSIONARY PRAYER

"I am moved by the many prayers offered here to give to the world the following prayer, which, if propagated and accepted by all people and every nation, will change the course of human events."

42

$\mathcal{I}$ choose with my free will to love God above all else, and my neighbor as myself. I choose this—Holy Love in the present moment—and seek God's help in doing so in every future moment. Amen.

Jesus' September 5, 2005 Monthly Message to All People and Every Nation

PRAYER TO INCREASE HOLY LOVE IN HEARTS

$\mathcal{D}$ear Jesus, increase the Holy Love in my heart just as You multiplied the loaves and fishes. Change my heart into a pure vessel of trust just as You changed the water into the best wine.

Look into my heart as You looked into the heart of the woman at the well, and remove any obstacle in my heart to Holy Love. Amen.

"In every instant, My Provision is complete and perfect. Nothing can be added or taken away by worry. The soul that trusts is at peace. Confidence in My Provision is always challenged by Satan. In order to increase your trust in Me, pray for an increase in Holy Love in your heart."

Jesus
December 26, 2007

PRAYER FOR ASSISTANCE WITH LIVING IN LOVE

*D*ear Heavenly Father, You are the Eternal Now. You created every present moment.

Help me to consecrate every present moment to Holy and Divine Love, for I understand it is only through Holy and Divine Love that mankind can be reconciled with his Creator. Amen.

"Do not presume, mankind, that you can overcome by yourself, obstacles to living in love. Ask for My assistance. Desire My assistance. It is only in and through grace, harmony with My Divine Will can return."
The Eternal Father—Father of All Creation
April 30, 2007

Obstacles To Living In Holy Love

Jesus: "This Mission of Holy Love is one of My Command Posts of Truth of the Remnant Faithful and of certain victory. Truth must be victorious in your hearts first and foremost. Therefore, pray to be enlightened as to any fault within your own heart, which presents itself as an obstacle to living in the truth of Holy Love. Such a prayer pleases Me."
(January 5, 2007 / Monthly Message to All People and Every Nation)

VICTORY PRAYER

*H*eavenly Father, I (*Name*), desire to be Your humble instrument in bringing about the Victory of the United Hearts. I understand that this Victory will be a Victory of Your Divine Will through Holy and Divine Love.

I wish to be a part of that Victory now, by living in Your Will in this present moment. I embrace the crosses You give me, for I know they are my strength in the journey towards Your Victory in my heart.

Remind me, Heavenly Father, that Your Victory will be ours, as well. It will be a Triumph of Love. Help me to be Your Love in the world. Amen.

Jesus
June 19, 2007

Ask For The Graces No One Wants

Our Lady: "Never neglect to ask Me, your Heavenly Mother, for the graces no one wants.
(April 19, 2008)

Daily Spiritual Practices

1. *A*ttend Mass and receive Holy Communion *(If Catholic) (See Chapter 4)*

   "If you are Catholic and listening to Me, I invite you to comprehend the most important part of your day should be Holy Mass."

   Jesus' November 5, 2003 Monthly Message
   to All People and Every Nation

2. *R*ecite the Rosary *(See Chapter 5)*

   "Once the soul begins daily recitation of the Rosary, the Blessed Mother pursues him—seeking his sanctity and deeper commitment to prayer."

   St. Thomas Aquinas
   October 7, 2002

3. *M*ake a Holy Hour before the Blessed Sacrament *(See Chapter 4)*

   "The practice of making a daily Holy Hour brings truth to light and scatters darkness."

   Jesus
   December 30, 2002

4. *M*editate on the Passion (See Chapter 6)

   "Meditate each day upon My Passion. Say the Stations of the Cross."

   Jesus
   June 24, 2001

Chapter 2. *Prayers To Overcome Faults*

****

In This Chapter:

****

"My brothers and sisters, you should be praying every day for enlightenment as to where your faults lie and how you can improve and come deeper into the Chambers of Our United Hearts. Do not be afraid to be shown where you are failing, for it is only in this way that you can improve, love Me more, love My Mother more and come deep into the deepest Chambers."

Jesus
January 17, 2005

PRAYER FOR VICTORY OF THE UNITED HEARTS

*D*ear Jesus, I know that the Victory of the United Hearts cannot come into the heart of the world unless it first comes into my own heart. Therefore, I ask that You give me the courage to look with the eyes of truth into my own heart to discover any area of inordinate self-love that I have not conquered. Take sovereignty over my heart.

Jesus, Triumph and Reign! Amen.

"This prayer is an important step in becoming an instrument towards Jesus' Victory instead of an obstacle."

St. Martin de Porres
November 28, 2007

CONSECRATION OF FAULTS TO DIVINE LOVE

*D*ear Jesus, Divine Love Incarnate, in this present moment I ask You to accept the surrender of all my faults. I consecrate every fault and weakness to Divine Love.

With this surrender I know You will show me more clearly what my faults are, why I give in to them, and You will give me strength to overcome them. Amen.

"Today I have come to help you realize the benefit of consecrating all your faults to Divine Love. In this act of consecration you will realize the root cause of your faults, which is the portal Satan uses to lead you astray; the nature of your faults; and the solution to overcoming each fault. This is the step each soul must take in order for Divine Love to become victorious in his heart."

St. Thomas Aquinas
August 31, 2005

PRAYER FOR HEALING WITH MARANATHA WATER
(While making the Sign of the Cross)

*D*ear Jesus, as I bless myself with this water, open my heart to the grace Heaven desires I have. Let me look into my soul with the eyes of truth. Give me the courage and humility to do so. Heal me according to the Will of Your Father. Amen.

"…My brothers and sisters, do not be surprised that in the healing prayer I imparted to the world this morning, I placed healing of the heart and soul first and foremost; for this is the main purpose of this Mission— the conversion of souls."

Jesus
January 18, 2008

PRAYER TO OVERCOME UNFORGIVENESS

Jesus, I trust in You. I know that You love me. I desire every obstacle between us be removed. Take from my heart any morsel of unforgiveness so that I can be completely Yours.

Help me to forgive those who have hurt me, have lied about me, have gossiped about me, were jealous of me, have stolen from me or have abused me in any way. Then plunge me deep into Your Most Sacred Heart. Cover Me with Your Most Precious Blood.

Do not allow me to resist Your Love again through unforgiveness of another. Amen.

"The Lord of Hosts says whole nations could benefit from this prayer."

Alanus (One of Maureen's Angels)

March 6, 2008

PRAYER TO PERFECT LOVE AND HUMILITY

Divine Heart of Jesus, in this present moment help me to live more deeply in Holy Love and Holy Humility. Give me the grace and the courage to look deep into my heart to see where I am failing in these virtues. I know it is only in overcoming these faults I can come deeper into the Chambers of Your Divine Heart. I beg Your strength in perfecting these virtues. Amen.

Jesus

August 3, 2002

Seek Mary As Refuge And Advocate

Jesus: "My brothers and sisters, today I advise you whenever you are challenged in Holy Love, seek the refuge of My Mother's Immaculate Heart. For it is flaws in Holy Love that result in lack of peace—even sin. My Mother, who is always your advocate, will take all your needs to My Heart in Heaven."

(April 5, 2008 / Monthly Message to All People and Every Nation)

REFLECTION ON PURGATORY
By Bishop Ignatius Horstmann
(Bishop of Cleveland, Ohio Diocese 1892-1908)

The Bishop comes. He says: "Praise be to Jesus."

"Jesus has allowed me to return to you to help the general public understand more about Purgatory itself. Purgatory is a cleansing grace. It is like the Flame of our Mother's Heart—Holy Love. Though it is painful, it cleanses the soul of all that is holding it back from a purer love. These are all venial sins. Or perhaps as in some cases, the soul has led a seriously sinful life, but at the last moment repents, and turning to God's mercy, is saved. Still, all that he has done needs to be atoned for. So then, Purgatory appeases the Heart of Divine Love for all the wounds afflicted upon it in this world."

51

"Even the one who sincerely attempts to lead a righteous life may have attitudes that he needs to atone for. Perhaps he is judgmental or unforgiving. He may adopt a negative attitude which does not account for God's grace. He may have deep-seated anger, which lays blame on others for his own faults. What I am saying is that **no soul should consider himself exempt from working to overcome his own shortcomings. If you do not work on them here, you will have to work on them in Purgatory. Everyone should look into their own hearts then, and ask for the grace to see their faults as God sees them. This is humility.**"

"God alone should make excuses for your faults. Learn to recognize Satan's lies, and do not fall victim to them. You will be given the grace you need to improve—always."

(July 21, 2006)

Purify Your Heart

Jesus: "My brothers and sisters, tonight I invite you to plunge your hearts into the purifying Flame of My Mother's Immaculate Heart. In order to be purified, you must recognize your own areas of weakness— your own faults. Pray for the grace to move your will in this direction. I welcome you into My Sacred Heart in every present moment."

(November 2, 2007)

Chapter 3. *Prayer Petitions For Personal Holiness*

* *

In This Chapter:

Prayer Posture for Petitions
Prayer Petitions

* *

PRAYER POSTURE FOR PETITIONS

Jesus, You are my strength.
Alone, I can do nothing.
Only You can fulfill this petition.

"Tonight I desire that you understand the proper prayer posture interiorly to have when you pray for a petition. When you desire that a petition be answered, My brothers and sisters, cast the petition upon the altar of My Sacred Heart. Place all your faith and hope and trust in the goodness of My Sacred Heart. Say to me [prayer]...And then leave the petition in My Heart. Every time it comes to mind, surrender it again in this manner. This pleases Me."

Jesus
September 19, 2005

53

PRAYER PETITIONS

TO DETACH FROM SELF AND TO BE FILLED AND CONSUMED WITH HOLY LOVE

Jesus: "The more the soul detaches from self, the more love of the Divine can fill his heart. Pray for this detachment. Pray to be filled and consumed with Holy Love. It is then the Kingdom of the Divine Will will be established in your heart."

(March 17, 2003)

TO BE PERFECTED IN LOVE

Jesus: "Pray to be perfected in love and you will have everything."

(September 2, 2003)

TO INCREASE IN FAITH, HOPE AND LOVE

St. Thomas Aquinas: "I have come to tell you that in order for the soul to increase in faith and hope, he must pray to increase in love, for love is the foundation of every virtue. If every other virtue were likened to the lyrics of a song, love would be the melody. If every other virtue were the ingredients in a loaf of bread, love would be the yeast."

"You see, then, that love is the passport to personal holiness, for without love all other virtues are false."

(October 15, 2007)

FOR DEEPER HUMILITY AND LOVE

Jesus: "My brothers and sisters, you are children of the Light; as such, I urge you to pray for deeper humility and love. The soul that embraces humility and love is the soul that can be repentant. It is the repentant heart that deserves My Mercy."

(April 21, 2006)

TO OVERCOME MISDIRECTED FREE WILL

Jesus: "My brothers and sisters, pray from the heart to overcome misdirected free will, for Heaven will be attentive to such a prayer. Then you will travel deeper into the Chambers of Our United Hearts."

(March 17, 2003)

FOR THE LIGHT TO SEE SMALL WAYS TO INCREASE IN CHILDLIKE HOLINESS

St. Thomas Aquinas comes and for the first time I notice all the buttons down the front of his cassock. He says: "Look at all these buttons your poor St. Thomas had to fasten every day. Yet, none of these were without eternal value, for I fastened each one with love for God and neighbor in my heart. Had I looked upon each one as a mundane chore, they would have been wasted."

"This is how to have the heart of a little child. Always carry the love of God in the center of your heart. Do everything, say everything, think everything

55

with this love. A child always trusts that his parents will make everything right. So the one who seeks childlike holiness must trust that the Will of God will bring good from every situation."

"The child takes joy from little things—a flower, a warm day—even a breeze to carry a kite. The childlike soul sees all the little things that God gives freely and rejoices in them."

"So you see, even buttons can add to your eternal happiness and carry you deeper into the Chambers of the United Hearts. Pray for the light to see small ways to increase in childlike holiness."

(April 19, 2005)

FOR THE GRACES NEEDED TO MOVE TOWARDS PERFECTION

Jesus: "If you desire deeper holiness, then you need to petition the Heart of My Most Immaculate Mother who is the Mediatrix of all grace to help you, to give you the graces that you need to move towards perfection. She will help you in unanticipated ways."

(August 7, 2006)

FOR A DEEP AND ABIDING LOVE OF THE FATHER'S DIVINE WILL

God the Father: "Dear child, no one can fathom the depths of My Divine Will any more than they can fathom

56

My Divine Mercy. But in the same way that Jesus petitions your heart to trust in Divine Mercy, I beg your trust in My Divine Will. Remember, trust is the fruit of love. Therefore, pray for a deep and abiding love of My Divine Will for you."

(February 28, 2007)

FOR THE STRENGTH TO BE HUMBLE OF HEART

Jesus: "My brothers and sisters, with a loving Heart I come tonight to warn you of a particular pitfall along the spiritual journey—that of false virtue. False virtue is practiced for others to see. False spirituality claims gifts that are not really present in the soul; take for instance, false discernment which leads people to believe Satan's lies. Pray for the strength to be humble of heart and you will avoid these pitfalls."

(March 23, 2007)

TO INCREASE MY LOVE
FOR THE HOLY TRINITY BY
THE POWER OF THE HOLY SPIRIT

Jesus: "Time is passing quickly as you know it now. So I invite you urgently to pray that the love you have in your heart for the Holy Trinity be increased by the power of the Holy Spirit, for it is the Holy Spirit who inspires every virtue and leads you deeper into the unity of Our United Hearts."

(May 5, 2007/ Monthly Message to
All People and Every Nation)

57

FOR EXTRA LOVE TO FACE TRIALS AND DIFFICULTIES

Jesus: "My brothers and sisters, whenever you are faced with a trial or some pending situation that will be difficult to handle, pray for extra love in your heart; for it is in this way you can overcome fear, which is the bad fruit of lack of trust. Lack of trust comes from imperfections in Holy Love. Pray always, My brothers and sisters, and I will assist you in your necessities."

(August 17, 2007)

TO STOP THINKING OF SELF

Jesus: "In your thoughts ask for the grace not to think of how everything affects you. It will be given. Ask, instead of thinking of self, to focus your thoughts on Me, on My Mother, on eternal life, on the lives of the saints and on the needs of others. This grace, too, shall be given."

(June 28, 2004)

TO INCREASE THE VIRTUE OF LOVE IN ME

Jesus: "My brothers and sisters, tonight I have come to tell you that just as the depth of your love measures the depth of your trust in Me, so too, the depth of your love measures the depth of your surrender to God's Divine Will. Therefore, pray every day the virtue of love be increased in you."

(May 4, 2007)

TO LOVE JESUS MORE IN THE NEXT PRESENT MOMENT THAN IN THIS ONE

Jesus: "My brothers and sisters, you will not disappoint Me or fail Me if you always hold in your heart the desire to love Me more in the next present moment than you do in this present moment. Such a human petition I will always grant with My favor."

(April 14, 2008)

FOR TRUE DISCERNMENT TO RECOGNIZE SATAN'S SNARES

Jesus: "Today, more than ever, all souls need the true gift of discernment so that they can recognize Satan and his insidious snares. I invite and I urge each soul to pray fervently for discernment daily. Do not presume you have this gift, but ask and you will recognize it when it is given."

(March 24, 2007)

FOR TRUTHFUL DISCERNMENT AND THE WISDOM TO UNDERSTAND THE UNITED HEARTS REVELATION

Jesus: "Further, I caution, human reason and intelligence will not help you understand the mystery of this Revelation of Our United Hearts. You must pray for truthful discernment and wisdom, which can come to you only from the Holy Spirit."

(February 25, 2007)

FOR A GENEROUS SPIRIT

St. Bernard of Clairvaux: "Listen carefully. I desire the world understand what I am about to say. The virtuous life—even grace itself—is often obstructed by human emotion. When people respond to situations, whether in thought, word or deed with purely emotion, virtue flees and so, too, does the grace to practice virtue."

"Say, for instance, someone offers constructive criticism to you and it is received only with lack of humility and self-defense. Perhaps you worry about your reputation and how others perceive your words or actions. This opposes simplicity of heart, which does not chase after its reputation. Perhaps you are prone to impatience or anger. Humility, based on Holy Love, must be allowed to capture your heart."

"Pray for a generous spirit. Such a spirit is always ready to forgive, always ready to practice virtue when put to the test. The generous heart recognizes when he should give to others and when to hold back. He recognizes the opportunities that grace affords him to practice virtue. In this way, he practices wisdom, not impulse."

"Always trust in the Lord to give you the grace you need to rise above pure human emotion. It is given to each soul in every present moment."

(April 14, 2008)

Chapter 4. **Mass And Eucharistic Adoration**

****

In this Chapter:

****

"But I have come to tell you what the adversary does not want you to hear; that is, that every Mass you attend, every Communion you receive, every Holy Hour you make, every prayer or Rosary you say, weakens the enemy forever in some soul somewhere in the world. This is the way to victory, little by little—one soul at a time patiently persevering in Holy Love."

Jesus' Monthly Message to All Nations
October 5, 2001

THE HOLY SACRIFICE OF THE MASS

COMMUNION PRAYER

*D*ear Jesus, as I approach Your altar to receive You in the Holy Eucharist, let me desire nothing but Divine Union with You.

Stand guard over my heart, defending me against all distractions and attacks against my Faith. Let me think of nothing but the great love You have for me—that You would come to me in so lowly a form as a piece of bread. Help me in my imperfect love to return love to You. Amen.

Jesus
March 11, 2005

PRAYER AFTER HOLY COMMUNION /
AS A SPIRITUAL COMMUNION

*D*ear Jesus, miraculously present in the Holy Eucharist, unite my heart to Your Eucharistic Heart. In this most precious moment when You are physically present in my heart, bring me into union with Divine Love, and hold me there always. Amen.

"I desire you recite this little prayer after Holy Communion. If you learn to recite it often throughout the day, it would also serve as a Spiritual Communion. It will

strengthen the Remnant Faithful. It is at communion the Lord finds rest in the temple of your heart."

Jesus

October 31, 2005

COMMUNION MEDITATIONS

St. Thomas Aquinas comes. He says: "Good day! Praise be to Jesus. Today I have come to give the world some meditations as they approach the Divine Presence in the sacrament of the Holy Eucharist."

1. "Imagine, if you will, Anna and Simeon in the temple awaiting the arrival of their Messiah. In their hearts they recognized His Divine Presence, as the young Mary carried Him into the temple. When you are about to receive Him—Body, Blood, Soul and Divinity—ask for the same grace—that you will recognize His Presence."

2. "Imagine the joy of the Wise Men and the shepherds when they came upon their Savior after following the star. Let grace be the 'star' that leads you to discover Jesus in the tabernacle."

3. "Imagine Blessed Mother's joy after searching for Her Son for three days when She comes upon Him speaking in the temple. Imagine Her love and exaltation as He placed His youthful Hand in Hers."

4. "Imagine John the Baptist in the womb of his mother—who, upon just hearing Mary's greeting as She approached—was sanctified."

5. "Finally, imagine Blessed Mother's joy as She was reunited with Her Beloved Son after He rose from the dead."

"Never receive the Holy Eucharist matter-of-factly. Approach Him with love and longing in your heart."
(January 28, 2003 / Feast of St. Thomas Aquinas)

REFLECTIONS ON THE MASS

Jesus: "When you come before Me, let it always be as though it were the first time, the first moment of your understanding of My Real Presence. When you receive Me, let it be as My Most Holy Mother received Me at the Annunciation. Ask for the grace. It is given. Ask for the grace to allow Me to stay within the tabernacle of your heart after you receive Me—to linger there—to languish in your soul. I delight in those that desire My Presence. Oh, how I do take delight in them! Believe and have faith that I choose it for each soul."
(July 16, 1999)

Jesus: "If you are Catholic and listening to Me, I invite you to comprehend the most important part of your day should be Holy Mass. Much preparation should precede

64

the prayer of the Mass, and much thanksgiving should follow it. Do not let others dictate to you your posture or demeanor in the precious moments after you receive Me in the Holy Eucharist. This is My special time with each soul and needs to be saturated with reciprocating love between the soul and Me. This moment in the interior forum must not be violated by community. Such a practice further reduces the importance of the sacrament of My Real Presence. When each soul is strengthened and nourished in this private moment with their Creator, the entire community will be strengthened. Do not fear putting into practice what I tell you today."

(November 5, 2003 / Monthly Message to
All People and Every Nation)

Our Lady: "Certain practices are being presented to you, My children, as favorable—even Vatican approved. The time after you receive the Sacred Eucharist is the special time between you and the Lord. Remember, in Holy Love we must love God above all else. This means He must be first. After My Son comes into your heart, it is a time for union with Divine Love. The Holy Father never asked you to stand and sing and be united with each other at this special moment of grace. These are all distractions. Do not be tricked into thinking otherwise. Do not relinquish this most cherished time with My Jesus to some avant-garde practice."

(October 31, 2005 / Message to the Remnant Faithful)

Jesus: "Just as I am physically present in the Eucharist, My Mother is spiritually present. If My Mother is spiritually present to you as you pray the Rosary, think how She must also be present spiritually as you receive Me in the Blessed Sacrament. My Mother stands guard over the tabernacles of the world. Is She not also guarding the tabernacle of your heart as you receive Me?"

(September 22, 1999)

Jesus: "When you receive Me under the form of the Eucharist, your heart becomes a tabernacle of Divine Love—Divine Mercy, for I am truly present in your heart during these moments just as I am truly present in the tabernacles of the world."

"It is during these precious moments in time that I cradle your soul in My Heart of hearts. I caress your petitions and press them into Divine Love. Treasure these moments as I do."

(April 23, 2001 / Conversation with Divine Love)

Jesus: "Understand, child, that when you receive Me under the humble form of the Holy Eucharist that you are receiving Divine Love. All of the Chambers of My Heart are open to you at that moment. Yet My Majesty remains humbly hidden, visible only to those who believe."

(January 19, 2000)

Jesus: "I come today to help you understand that My Sacred Heart and My Eucharistic Heart are One. Since

My Eucharistic Sacred Heart is Divine Love, each time you receive this Sacred Species, you are receiving a little Spark of the Flame of Divine Love. How I desire to keep this Spark alive in each heart always!"

(December 2, 2002)

Jesus: "The closest any soul can come to Me is in the reception of the Holy Eucharist. Let every Mass be an advent then, in anticipation of My coming."
(December 5, 2002 / Monthly Message to the Remnant Faithful)

St. Thomas Aquinas: "Through the Eucharist, the Will of God is present in the world—completely, perfectly and eternally. Then, understand that the Fifth Chamber—union with the Divine Will—is offered to each one who partakes of the Holy Eucharist."

(February 8, 2003)

Jesus: "My brothers and sisters, when you receive Me under the form of bread and wine in the Most Holy Eucharist of the altar, you receive in entirety My Body, Blood, Soul and Divinity. It is only when a soul gives in to any form of pride that I leave his heart. Long to be with Me, as I long to be with you."

(June 22, 2003 / Feast of Corpus Christi)

Jesus: "My brothers and sisters, today I come to remind you that the Holy Eucharist is a Sacrament of Love. In this Sacrament, your love for Me and My Love for you unite and become one. I want to make of your hearts shining lights of Divine Love in the world."

(April 29, 2005)

EUCHARISTIC ADORATION

BENEFITS OF EUCHARISTIC ADORATION

Jesus: "But I have come to you seeking your assistance. I need each one's cooperation with grace. Pray your Rosaries and ask for peace in hearts. Make holy hours of reparation before My Real Presence."

"Here are the benefits of one holy hour well-made:"

Benefits

1. "When you lay your petitions at the foot of the altar, angels carry them to Heaven."

2. **"When you make a holy hour and then recite an Our Father, Hail Mary and All Glory Be for the intentions of the Holy Father, the punishment due your sins is remitted. Or, if you offer these same prayers, but give the graces earned to a poor soul in Purgatory, he will be released."**

3. "The practice of making a daily holy hour brings truth to light and scatters darkness."

4. "I draw into My Sacred Heart those who esteem My

Real Presence. They will be drawn quickly through the Chambers of the United Hearts. I will convict their consciences, making it difficult for them to resist Me."

(December 30, 2002)

REFLECTIONS ON EUCHARISTIC ADORATION

Jesus: "In truth I tell you, there is no beginning nor end to this holy hour you offer Me. It began before time began and it reaches into eternity. My Father's Will encapsulates it just as it embraces every present moment."

(January 25, 2005)

St. Martin de Porres: "Dear sister, I have come to offer you this message. Please know and understand the great consolation Jesus feels in His Divine Heart whenever you pray before His Real Presence. As He is consoled, the stranglehold that Satan has upon the throat of the world is loosened, and souls are given knowledge as to their sinful ways..."

"Believe that one holy hour can save a soul and change the course of human history forever. Live as though you believe this profound truth."

(November 25, 2006)

Jesus: "When you honor Me in this hidden form of the Holy Eucharist, I am pleased to take all of your petitions and lay them upon the altar of My Heart. You have no need or concern that escapes Me."

(February 5, 2004 / Monthly Message to All People and Every Nation)

Jesus is standing by the tabernacle when I enter the chapel. He has a large host over His Heart with a bright light radiating from it. He says, "I desire people adore My Eucharistic Heart. I am Jesus, born of the flesh. As I came to earth clothed in humanity, understand I am still with you clothed in bread and wine. If people really believed in Me, this chapel would be overflowing. But truly I tell you, the time will come when this will be so. The confessionals will be full again, the churches filled to overflowing. How I languish in hopeful love as these times approach! I hold dear those who come to Me now to comfort Me in faith and love."

"Make this known."

(July 1, 1999 / Feast of the Precious Blood)

Jesus: "When you begin to see tabernacles restored to their rightful place in the Churches, and Eucharistic Adoration esteemed by all, you will know My victory is at hand."

(August 7, 2002)

Chapter 5. *Rosary Prayers And Meditations*

∗∗

In This Chapter:

∗∗

PRAYER OF PETITION TO LIVE IN THE DIVINE WILL

Heavenly Father, during this time of world crisis, let all souls find their peace and security in Your Divine Will. Give each soul the grace to understand that Your Will is Holy Love in the present moment.

Benevolent Father, illuminate each conscience to see the ways that he is not living in Your Will. Grant the world the grace to change and the time in which to do it. Amen.

"Ask your country to pray this prayer. Begin with My Missionary Servants of Holy Love."

"This prayer should be recited at the beginning of the Rosary and before the Creed. Besides that, it needs to be propagated far and wide. I charge My Missionary Servants of Holy Love with this task."

Mary, Mother of God
September 28, 2001
(After the 9/11 Terrorist Attack on the USA)

PRAYER TO BE RECITED WITH THE ROSARY OF THE UNBORN

(Please see Chapter 15)

ROSARY MEDITATIONS
Dictated by Maureen's Guardian Angel
September 14, 2001
(After the 9/11 Terrorist Attack on the USA)

Joyful Mysteries

ANNUNCIATION

You said 'yes' to the angel without regard to cost to Yourself, Blessed Mother. Help us to say 'yes' to God's will for us in every present moment. Sorrowful and Immaculate Heart of Mary, Pray For Us.

$\mathcal{V}$ISITATION

You traveled to visit Your cousin and to assist her in her need. Protect us on our journeys from any terrorist attacks. Sorrowful and Immaculate Heart of Mary, Pray For Us.

$\mathcal{N}$ATIVITY

You were unable to find a suitable dwelling place for the birth of Your Son, Mary. Yet, Jesus nestled in Your arms must have felt secure. Help us as a nation to feel secure once more. Sorrowful and Immaculate Heart of Mary, Pray For Us.

$\mathcal{P}$RESENTATION

Your heart was pierced by a sword, Mary, so that the thoughts of many would be laid bare. Our hearts are pierced today, Blessed Mother, as we see the evil that was behind these terrorist attacks. Sorrowful and Immaculate Heart of Mary, Pray For Us.

$\mathcal{F}$INDING JESUS IN THE TEMPLE

When Jesus was lost You searched for Him sorrowing, Blessed Mother. Many are lost today as a result of this attack on our country. We ask You to assist those who search for them, and those who wait for them with the grace of Your heart. Sorrowful and Immaculate Heart of Mary, Pray For Us.

Sorrowful Mysteries

AGONY IN THE GARDEN

Jesus, You agonized over those who would not turn to You despite Your death on the cross. Jesus, we ask You to have mercy on the terrorists who will not turn to You. Sacred Heart of Jesus, Have Mercy On Us.

SCOURGING AT THE PILLAR

Your flesh was torn from Your bones, Jesus. Many suffered injuries in these terrorist attacks. Sacred Heart of Jesus, Have Mercy On Us.

CROWNING WITH THORNS

So many suffer mental anguish over these senseless acts of violence, Jesus. Help this nation as it mourns. Sacred Heart of Jesus, Have Mercy On Us.

CARRYING OF THE CROSS

You accepted Your cross with patience, Jesus. Help our nation to bear patiently this heavy cross. Sacred Heart of Jesus, Have Mercy On Us.

CRUCIFIXION

As You embraced Your cross, Jesus, You prayed for Your enemies. Help us to forgive our enemies and to pray for them. Sacred Heart of Jesus, Have Mercy On Us.

Glorious Mysteries

*R*ESURRECTION

Help us as a nation to rise from the ashes of this tragedy. Sacred Heart of Jesus, Have Mercy On Us.

*A*SCENSION

You ascended to Your throne in Heaven, Jesus, victorious over death. From Your throne, take into Heaven all who have perished in this tragedy. Sacred Heart of Jesus, Have Mercy On Us.

*D*ESCENT OF THE HOLY SPIRIT

Our bodies are meant to be temples of the Holy Spirit. Inspire all people and every nation to respect life from conception to natural death. Sacred Heart of Jesus, Have Mercy On Us.

*A*SSUMPTION

Mary, You were assumed into Heaven body and soul because Your heart was blameless before God. Please pray that the heart of our nation becomes blameless before God by overturning abortion. Immaculate Heart of Mary, Pray For Us.

*C*ORONATION

From Your throne in Heaven, Mary, You can see into all hearts. Reveal to us our enemies. Inspire our nation's leaders to reconcile the heart of this nation to God. Immaculate Heart of Mary, Pray For Us.

THE LUMINOUS MYSTERIES OF THE ROSARY
Dictated by Jesus on November 2, 2002

BAPTISM OF JESUS

When I was about to begin My public ministry, I received a baptism in the river Jordan. The sky opened and the Holy Spirit descended upon Me. Today, the Heavens are opening once again. This time The Fire of Divine Love is pouring down upon earth seeking to engulf every heart with a Pentecost of Love. Each one should make it his personal mission to spread this Flame.

WEDDING AT CANA

My Mother holds no petition in Her Heart that She does not turn over to Me and place in My Sacred Heart. In all things Mary is the Perfect Intercessor and Advocate. When the soul turns to Her with a need She adds Her own prayer to it and gives it to Me. See this sign I worked at the wedding feast as a sign that Our Hearts are, indeed, <u>united</u>.

PROCLAMATION OF THE KINGDOM

My Mercy and My Love are one; they are Divine, Perfect and Eternal. They never fail. The soul that trusts in My Love and Mercy is the one I am able to forgive. The kingdom begins in every heart that begins to believe in My Love and Mercy. This is how a conversion of heart takes place. This is My Victory.

THE TRANSFIGURATION

The joy of the miracle of the Transfiguration took place so as to anchor the apostles in faith. At My Mother's authentic apparition sites, such as the one at Holy Love, miracles abound so as to support the message that is given. Those who are bold enough to doubt a bodily apparition must wonder, then, at the account of the Transfiguration where Moses and Elijah appeared on either side of Me. Have faith!

THE INSTITUTION OF THE EUCHARIST

I gave My Body and Blood in the first Eucharist, and I give them continually today in every Mass throughout the world. This sacrament is strength for the journey through the Chambers of Our United Hearts. Too often My Love and Mercy go unattended. I am ignored and set aside in Churches. I am blasphemed by those who receive Me unworthily. I am received lukewarmly by <u>most,</u> and even some priests. Pray this mystery in atonement to My Eucharistic Heart.

REFLECTION ON THE ROSARY

St. Thomas Aquinas comes. He bows before the tabernacle and says: "Praise be to Jesus."

"The Holy Mother has sent me to talk to you about the Rosary. Some people—even Church leaders—make light of it, you know. But the power of the Rosary has not changed over the centuries. If more would pray it, abortion would be recognized for what it is. The acceptance of abortion by any country's leaders places the country in jeopardy; for this sin alone brings about wars, natural disasters, political confusion and economic collapse."

"Devotion to the Holy Rosary places the soul under the Blessed Mother's protection—certainly a place anyone should seek to be during these times. Carrying the rosary with you is a sign to Satan that you belong to Mary."

"Meditation upon the mysteries of the Rosary brings the soul closer to Jesus, and leads him away from sin. The Rosary is a decisive weapon against Satan's kingdom in this world."

"Once the soul begins daily recitation of the Rosary, the Blessed Mother pursues him—seeking his sanctity and deeper commitment to prayer."

"Make this known."

(October 7, 2002)

The Family Rosary

Our Lady: "I desire that families unite under the banner of the Holy Rosary once again."

April 19, 2008

Chapter 6. *Meditating On The Passion*

****

In This Chapter:

The Stations of the Cross
When You Meditate on My Passion
Dictations on My Passion and Death
    Agony in the Garden
    Scourging at the Pillar
    Crowning with Thorns
    Carrying of the Cross
    Crucifixion and Death on the Cross
    Descent to the Dead
    My Passion Continues Today
Lessons from the Passion

****

"...I have come today to invite you to meditate daily upon My Passion, for such a meditative prayer stirs in your heart sentiments of love and compassion for Me. Every moment that you give Me in love, I return to you a hundredfold through Divine Love in this life and in the next."

Jesus
September 10, 2000

STATIONS OF THE CROSS

1. Jesus is Condemned to Death
2. Jesus Accepts His Cross
3. Jesus Falls the First Time
4. Jesus Meets His Mother
5. Simon Carries the Cross
6. Veronica Wipes the Face of Jesus
7. Jesus Falls the Second Time
8. Jesus Consoles the Women of Jerusalem
9. Jesus Falls a Third Time
10. Jesus is Stripped of His Garments
11. Jesus is Nailed to the Cross
12. Jesus Dies on the Cross
13. Jesus is Taken Down from the Cross
14. Jesus is Laid in the Tomb

Holy Love Is The Tenth Station

Jesus: "Holy Love is the Tenth Station of the Cross. It is stripping yourself of all that stands between you and salvation. It is dying to your own will. In Holy Love, there is only one will, one opinion that matters, and that is God's. Sanctification comes when the soul can see what stands between himself and God, and he strips himself of it. It is My Tenth Station."

(September 30, 1994)

WHEN YOU MEDITATE ON MY PASSION
Messages from Jesus

"Contemplate My wounds, for to do so appeases My Heart. When you meditate on My Passion and death you are able to overcome Satan's temptations in the present moment."

(September 11, 2000)

"Dear child, when you meditate on My Passion the fairness of My Father's Mercy pours out in abundance upon humanity. I am then able to draw closer to souls who do not know Me or recognize Me."

"My Father's plan—His Will—is eternal and always at work in the world. It goes unacknowledged and unacclaimed by most, but never departs from its course."

"When you meditate therefore on My Blessed Passion, you bring it to life. You are Veronica wiping My Face. You are Simon helping Me to carry the Cross. You are standing with My Mother at the foot of the Cross, consoling Her. You are affirming the Divine Will in the world."

(November 3, 2000 / Conversation with Divine Love)

"When you meditate upon My Passion and Death, I take you deeper in the Flame of Divine Love. When you meditate upon My Mother's Passion, I owe you My gratitude."

(May 5, 2004 / Conversation with Divine Love)

"When you meditate upon My Passion and Death, you bring to Me contrite hearts. Never fail Me in this, then. Mercy begets mercy. When you give Me contrite hearts by your efforts, I will never fail you in My Mercy."

(Jesus' February 5, 2002
Monthly Message to All Nations)

"Please understand that much of My Passion took place within My Heart. I mourned for the souls that would be lost despite My sacrifice. My Heart was moved with pity for the self-righteous and arrogant. These are the ones who feel they are on the path of salvation as they slip to their perdition."

"As I suffered, My Mother suffered the Passion within Her own Heart—feeling not only physical pain but the agony of the loss of souls. Besides all of this, She suffered the pain of separation from Me—though mystically Our Hearts were united even in the darkest hour."

"This is why the Flame of My Heart so willingly engulfs the soul that meditates upon My Passion and Death. This is why I am gracious towards those who meditate upon the sorrows of My Mother."

(May 14, 2004 / Conversation with Divine Love)

DICTATIONS ON MY PASSION AND DEATH
Messages from Jesus

AGONY IN THE GARDEN

"Child, I desire to share with you facts about My Passion and Death that have heretofore remained hidden…"

"First I will take you to the Garden of Gethsemane. I moved towards this point in time with a heavy Heart—heavy, for I knew so many would slip to their perdition despite My sacrifice. The greatest suffering I bore for the redemption of mankind was the Divine Knowledge of the lack of love in hearts. Many times during persecutions, you feel only a fraction of My sorrow; but imagine if you experienced all the hate and apathy of every human heart that ever existed or ever will exist—all at once!"

"This is what caused the Blood to flow from My Pores. This is why I begged that this Chalice be passed by Me. When I accepted My Father's Will, I did not receive any consolation of knowing His approval. An angel came and ministered to Me by cleansing the Blood which had fallen…"

(February 19, 2005 / Conversation with Divine Love)

SCOURGING AT THE PILLAR

"The Chambers of Our United Hearts remained open throughout My Passion. I was willing to welcome and forgive any one of My torturers if they would but turn to Me with a remorseful heart. None did. Darkness overshadowed them. They did not recognize Me, just as many do not recognize Me today in the Holy Eucharist."

"The insults of the whips were not easy to bear, but I had surrendered to the Will of My Father. Therefore, I bore every blow for mankind's redemption. These pains were little compared to the pain of seeing the hearts of My persecutors. Their hearts were vessels of apathy, hatred and disgust. How many today carry the same spirits in their hearts?"

"My Mother suffered each blow in Her own Body mystically that I suffered physically. I could not protect Her from this trial which was a bitter portion of My Passion and Death."

"Today it is the prayers of Her consecrated children that support My Mother as She looks into the hearts of mankind. Do not fail Her, for She suffers much."

(March 4, 2005 / Conversation with Divine Love)

CROWNING WITH THORNS

"The Crowning with Thorns which I suffered at the hand of My torturers had particular significance. Each thorn represented the prideful worship of a false god in the hearts of My persecutors—then and now and in the future."

"There was the thorn of the false god of wealth which penetrated the deepest. This thorn was closely challenged by the false god of reputation. Then there was the false god of physical beauty. I must not neglect the thorn of the false god of intellect."

"The Crown of Thorns was particularly difficult to bear for it mirrored so closely the errors in the hearts of men. While I suffered with love in My Heart, My torturers attacked Me with venomous hatred. Their love of God had been replaced by disordered self-love. I bled for them."

(March 11, 2005 / Conversation with Divine Love)

"My brothers and sisters, see and understand that the thorn which penetrated the deepest into My Head represented the souls who say they love Me but do not trust Me. Oh! How often this happens, and often to the souls that I have been the closest to. Consider My anguish and then see that your love and trust must be united as Our Hearts are united."

(February 28, 2005)

CARRYING OF THE CROSS

"Today I have come to speak to you about My carrying of the Cross—a journey which led to the sacrifice of sacrifices. Humanly, I could not have made this journey as I was already greatly weakened by previous trials. It was by merit of My Mother's prayers I was able to bear up under this burden. I kept My focus on the souls who would succeed in passing through the narrow gates

85

of Paradise because of My sacrifice. I could not think of Myself. The moments when I was most vulnerable to Satan's attacks to reject these trials are the ones I surrendered to the Father for those who allow Satan to usurp them in the corruption of others."

(March 18, 2005 / Conversation with Divine Love)

CRUCIFIXION AND DEATH ON THE CROSS

"On this day so many hundreds of years long past, salvation mounted the Cross. Yes, Love and Mercy made one—suffered and died for all and for each one. My pain was made more intense when I looked upon My Sorrowing Mother. Still today—for there is no time or space in Heaven—you can console My Mother as She stands at the foot of the Cross."

"My consolation as I hung dying was the knowledge of the Divine Mercy devotion in these latter days, and the spread of the Confraternity of the United Hearts. The Confraternity opens the font of Divine Love that is My Heart for all to share. It is through knowledge of the Chambers of Our United Hearts souls will be assisted in their mount to perfection and will be able to find, and to imitate Divine Love."

"I held nothing back on Calvary. I surrendered all for the sake of sinners. Each of you must decide to surrender everything to Me in order to be free to choose for Holy and Divine Love."

"No pain I suffered on the Cross was too great, for

I beheld the face of humanity before Me. I suffer still when I see any sinner turn away from Me. I implore you—imitate Divine Love and Divine Mercy to one another. I will reach down from the Cross and help you."

(March 25, 2005 / Good Friday
Conversation with Divine Love)

"As I drew in My last breath on the Cross—My dying prayer—My last thought was for My Church upon earth."

(August 7, 2002)

"As I drew in My last breath—a breath that caused Me excruciating pain—I was consoled by the knowledge that two Revelations would draw My Remnant Faithful together. One was the Revelation of My Divine Mercy —the other was the Revelation of the Chambers of Our United Hearts."

(April 18, 2003 / Good Friday – 3:00 p.m.)

"As I underwent My Passion and death, I saw this Mission take form and it was a great consolation."

(February 17, 2000)

DESCENT TO THE DEAD

"After My death on the Cross, I descended to a place which was neither Hell nor Purgatory—a place where many awaited Me—the patriarchs—Moses, My foster

87

father Joseph, to name a few. Before I released them to enter the glory of Heaven, I charged each one of them to pray for My Love and Mercy to be made known in these last days."

"I bid them pray for the Divine Mercy Revelation and for the Confraternity of the United Hearts—the two vehicles of My Divine Love and Divine Mercy. I made them understand that these vehicles of My Love and Mercy would convert and save a multitude before My return. Then I sent them to Heaven."

(March 26, 2005 / Holy Saturday
Conversation with Divine Love)

*M*Y PASSION CONTINUES TODAY

"My brothers and sisters, My Passion continues today in the form of every murder that is committed, every abortion that is performed. It continues in all those who scorn the Christian ideal of Holy Love. And so I invite you tonight to remember Me as I remembered you in My Passion."

(September 11, 2000)

"You ponder, child, how it is the errant soul still causes Me to suffer, and how your sacrifices today can alleviate My Passion. In Heaven there is no time or space. Therefore, I still suffer for every sin committed and I am always victorious in every heart that is converted."
(September 21, 2000 / Conversation with Divine Love)

"It is within the Fourth Chamber of My Heart that I experience My Passion and death as every Mass is celebrated." (February 7, 2000)

"You may wonder, My daughter, at My revealing to you certain sorrows in certain Chambers of My Heart. But it is true, that certain sorrows thrust the sword of suffering deeper into My Heart than any. My greatest sorrow, the one that bitterly occupies the Fourth Chamber of My Heart, is the sacrileges and outrages that I suffer in My Real Presence in the tabernacles of the world." (February 7, 2000)

"Today, I come to you to describe to the world My Wounds."

"The Wounds of My Hands were suffered for those who embrace evil and oppose righteousness. With Me there is no half-measure. You are either for Me or against Me."

"The Wounds of My Feet were suffered for those who once walked in righteousness, but have strayed from the path."

"The Wound of My Heart was suffered for priests— the lukewarm priests—those who have compromised or forsaken their vocation—those who offer the Holy Sacrifice of the Mass with sullied hands."

"All of these I suffered for the salvation of souls, and I suffer them still today." (April 18, 2003 / Good Friday)

LESSONS FROM THE PASSION

Jesus: "Please understand that as I suffered My Passion, I could have called a brigade of angels to My defense, but I chose to suffer in silence. I prayed as I suffered that My enemies would be convicted in their hearts of their sins. You must do the same for this is unconditional love."

(February 25, 2005 / Conversation with Divine Love)

Jesus: "My brothers and sisters, many times in the days preceding My Passion and Death, I was overcome with fear of what was to befall Me. But once I accepted the Cross, thereby surrendering to it, I was given the strength and the courage to bear it. You must do likewise."

(April 10, 2006)

St. Margaret Mary Alacoque: "Jesus' surrender in Gethsemane was complete and perfect. Yet, He had to continually surrender to His Father's Will throughout His Passion. This is because Satan tried to tempt Him to come down from the Cross. It is no different in the moment to moment surrender that each soul gives to Jesus. Satan tries to tempt the soul into rejecting the cross—the greater the cross, the greater the temptation."

"Remember, Jesus had angels minister to Him after His surrender to His Father's Will. Each soul has his guardian angel next to him helping him to surrender, and supporting him in the face of each temptation to abandon his surrender."

"Jesus desires that you seek the shelter of your angels' wings in living out these Messages of Holy and Divine Love, which is God's Divine Will."

(October 27, 2007)

Jesus: "As I underwent My Passion and death, my great consolation was that I would remain in the world clothed in the Eucharist. Not that I wanted to cling to the world or life in the world, but as My Father's Will, I remain as a strength and support to all of humanity."

"Yes, I am here! I am present—Body, Blood, Soul and Divinity. The only thing that can loosen my spiritual bond with all people is free will. Therefore, I come to say—believe in Me truly present in the tabernacles of the world."

(April 12, 2001 / Holy Thursday)

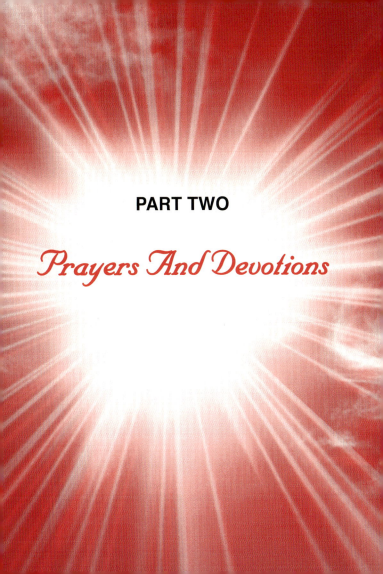

PART TWO

Prayers And Devotions

Chapter 7. *Acts Of Consecration*

* *

In This Chapter:

* *

"So today I come to you, telling you to be consecrated to the truth—the truths of the Tradition of Faith, the truths of the Ten Commandments, the truth of My Laws of Holy Love.

Jesus
February 5, 2008
Monthly Message to All People and Every Nation

CONSECRATION TO SELF-DENIAL

*D*ear Jesus, Divine and Beloved Savior, today I surrender to You every pain—physical, spiritual or emotional. I will not complain about inconveniences, demands upon my time, breaches of privacy or the rudeness of those You put in my life today. With Your help, I will accept each present moment with Holy Love. Amen.

"The reason the Lord sent me to you with that morning prayer is, if you recite it in the morning, then great and small sacrifices that you may forget to offer the Lord have already been given to Him."

St. Martin de Porres
November 3, 2006

CONSECRATION TO THE DIVINE WILL

*H*eavenly Father, I desire that You place the Seal of Your Divine Will upon my heart. Thus, I will accept Your Will in all situations and in every present moment. I will accept all things as from Your Hand for the good of my salvation and the salvation of others. Amen.

Two Angels adoring Jesus at Adoration
October 15, 2001

CONSECRATION TO HOLY LOVE IN THE PRESENT MOMENT

*H*eavenly Father, I consecrate my heart in this present moment to Holy Love. Keep me mindful of this throughout the day so that all my thoughts and actions will proceed from Holy Love."

I cover this petition with the Most Precious Blood of Jesus, your Son, and surround it with the Tears of His Most Sorrowful Mother. Amen.

St. Thomas Aquinas
January 21, 2002

PRAYER FOR ASSISTANCE WITH LIVING IN LOVE

*D*ear Heavenly Father, You are the Eternal Now. You created every present moment.

Help me to consecrate every present moment to Holy and Divine Love, for I understand it is only through Holy and Divine Love that mankind can be reconciled with his Creator. Amen.

"Do not presume, mankind, that you can overcome by yourself, obstacles to living in love. Ask for My assistance. Desire My assistance. It is only in and through grace, harmony with My Divine Will can return."

The Eternal Father—Father of All Creation
April 30, 2007

PRAYER OF CONSECRATION TO THE TRUTH

*Y*our words, Lord, are Light and Truth. Your Provision, Your Mercy and Your Love come to me clothed in truth.

Help me always to live in Your Truth. Assist me in recognizing Satan's deceit in my own thoughts and in the thoughts, words and actions of others. Do not let humility elude me, as I know humility is truth itself. Amen.

Jesus
July 13, 2007

CONSECRATION OF FAULTS TO DIVINE LOVE

*D*ear Jesus, Divine Love Incarnate, in this present moment I ask You to accept the surrender of all my faults. I consecrate every fault and weakness to Divine Love.

With this surrender I know You will show me more clearly what my faults are, why I give in to them, and You will give me strength to overcome them. Amen.

"Today I have come to help you realize the benefit of consecrating all your faults to Divine Love. In this act of consecration you will realize the root cause of your faults, which is the portal Satan uses to lead you astray; the nature of your faults; and the solution to overcoming each fault. This is the step each soul must take in order

for Divine Love to become victorious in his heart."

St. Thomas Aquinas
August 31, 2005

CHILDREN'S CONSECRATION TO THE UNITED HEARTS

*D*ear United Hearts of Jesus and Mary, I love You very much. I want to give You this present moment and all the future moments of my life. I always want to please You. I give You my heart today and always, and pray You will unite it to Your United Hearts.

Place in my heart, dear Jesus and Mary, the desire to help sinners turn to You. Amen.

"Copy this prayer to the United Hearts. It can serve as a consecration of children to the Two Hearts. Propagate it among the young."

St. Margaret Mary Alacoque
October 12, 2006

FAMILY CONSECRATION TO THE UNITED HEARTS
According to St. Thomas Aquinas

(Please see Chapter 17 for the Family Consecration Ceremony)

OFFERING OF PAST CROSSES

(Please see Chapter 12 for the conditions for consecrating all past crosses.)

CONSECRATION TO THE EUCHARISTIC HEART FOR PRIESTS

My Jesus, Divine Good, accept my heart as Your instrument in the world through Holy Love, which is the Immaculate Heart of Mary. I consecrate my vocation in this present moment to Your Eucharistic Heart. I will dedicate my life to bringing the Holy Eucharist to those You lead me to, and to whom I am led.

I desire union and faithfulness to the Will of the Eternal Father through consecration to Your Eucharistic Heart. Amen.

Jesus
May 31, 2005

CONSECRATION OF NATIONS TO GOD'S DIVINE WILL

I, (*Name*), as leader of this nation of _____, desire to consecrate this country to God's Divine Will which is Love and Mercy itself. I realize that the future of this nation depends upon Divine Mercy and Divine Love.

I resolve to avoid offending God's Will in any way through supporting legislation which is contrary to His Love and Mercy, or in taking any diplomatic measure which transgresses human rights. I surrender the future to God's Will and His Provision. Amen.

"I have come so that the leaders of every nation can put this prayer to use."

Jesus
May 29, 2006

CONSECRATION OF THE WORLD TO THE UNITED HEARTS
(To be recited by Church Leaders)

Heavenly Father, in this present moment, which You have created and willed, I _____*(name)*_____, do hereby consecrate the heart of this country, _____*(name)*_____ to the United Hearts of the Holy Trinity in union with the Immaculate Heart of Mary.

Dictated by God the Father
September 18, 2007

(Please see Chapter 14 for Messages about this worldwide consecration)

PART TWO: PRAYERS AND DEVOTIONS

Chapter 8. *Blessings*

****

In This Chapter:

Blessings from Heaven
Passing a Blessing to Others
Blessing of Paternal Love
Complete Blessing of the United Hearts

****

BLESSINGS FROM HEAVEN

In 2007, Heaven imparted to the world two new Blessings which can be passed on to individuals and to groups:

Blessing of Paternal Love

Complete Blessing of the United Hearts

These are in addition to the five blessings imparted by Heaven in the 1980s and 1990s.

Blessing of the United Hearts

Blessing of Holy Love

Blessing of Divine Love

Blessed Mother's Special Blessing

Blessed Mother's Motherly Blessing

Combined Graces

The Blessings all carry the same benefits, as summarized below. However, the Paternal Love Blessing is of particular merit to the Poor Souls, and the Complete Blessing of the United Hearts hastens Jesus' Victory in hearts.

When you give or receive one of the Blessings:

1. It will gratify the most distant heart and bring them closer to Jesus.

2. It will strengthen spiritually and often physically.

3. It is preparing mankind for Jesus' Second Coming.

4. It carries with it special graces of healing—both spiritual and physical.

5. It will be a deterrent to Satan and bring with it disclosure of evil in hearts and in the world.

6. It will draw everyone who receives it to a devotion of the United Hearts.

7. It enables one to live in the virtue of Holy Love.

8. It is a strength in adversity, patience amidst trial.

9. It is a deepening in the virtues that you are called to through the Blessing, once you surrender.

10. It brings with it the grace of zeal for holiness.

11. It extends over you and in you abundant grace to choose the Divine Will in every present moment.

12. It gives peace.

13. It assists the soul in carrying his cross and mitigates Divine Justice through the cross.

14. It inspires souls to come closer to the Paternal Love of the Father.

PASSING A BLESSING TO OTHERS

These seven Blessings are all transferable to others, so pass them on! Keep it simple. Merely think or speak or write:

I extend to you (Name) the (Name of the Blessing).

(e.g., I extend to you and to the world the Complete Blessing of the United Hearts.)

When You Pass A Blessing

"I am your Jesus, born Incarnate. Children, understand that when you pass a blessing—any blessing—to another, it is the faith and love in your hearts that determines the strength of the blessing. This is so with all prayer and every blessing that you offer on behalf of another. Every promise attendant to the blessings you have been given here at this site— United Hearts, Holy Love, Divine Love, Special Blessing and Motherly Love—come alive through the strength of the faith and love in your hearts when it is offered."

"Make it known."

(February 16, 2001)

BLESSING OF PATERNAL LOVE

Once again I see a great Flame which I know to be the Heart of God the Father. He says: "I am Paternal Love—the Eternal Now."

"I come to give this generation encouragement. The crosses I permit in your lives are signs of My Victory. Through the Heart of the Immaculata, you will be given all the grace you need to cooperate with each cross and be victorious in Love."

"Always remember that the Blessing of My Paternal Love is with you in every present moment. My Blessing rests gently upon the hearts of this generation, waiting to be accepted and acknowledged. If souls turn to Me, it is within My Power to circumvent evil plans that the enemy has placed in hearts. Every precious present moment counts."

"I extend to you and to the world the Blessing of My Paternal Love."

Graces

Then, Jesus comes. He says: "I am your Jesus, born Incarnate."

"I come to tell you the graces attendant to the Blessing of Paternal Love that the Father has just revealed to you."

1. "Those who come to the property experience this Blessing if their hearts are open, and if they accept the Messages of Holy and Divine Love. It gives peace."

2. "The Blessing of Paternal Love assists the soul in carrying his cross and mitigates Divine Justice through the cross. Thus, you should pass this Blessing on to the Poor Souls in Purgatory."

(July 24, 2007)

COMPLETE BLESSING OF
THE UNITED HEARTS

Jesus: "…We are blessing you now with THE COMPLETE BLESSING OF THE UNITED HEARTS— FATHER, SON, HOLY SPIRIT AND IMMACULATE MARY."

(First imparted on August 5, 2007 in Jesus' Monthly Message to All People and Every Nation)

Graces

Jesus: "My brothers and sisters, **as the new Complete Blessing of the United Hearts is given on a regular basis here at the Prayer Site, souls will feel inspired to come closer to the Paternal Love of My Father**. But this call will need to be protected; and so, I am asking My foster father, Joseph, to protect hearts and this inspiration to know the Father better."

(August 6, 2007)

Chapter 9. Invocations And Ejaculatory Prayers

* *

In This Chapter:

* *

TRUST EJACULATION

*E*ternal Father, I trust in Your loving Will for me.

"*Do not be quick to question circumstances and events of the day, but see My Will in every present moment. Carry in your heart and upon your lips, the ejaculation, '**Eternal Father, I trust in Your loving Will for me.**' This little prayer carries with it—peace. I send an angel to assist you when you believe.*"

"I, your Eternal Father, desire this be made known and be made popular."

Eternal Father
February 28, 2007

MANKIND'S BATTLE CRY

God's Will be done.

"Today the battle cry of all mankind needs to be **'God's Will be done**.*' This is the way to surrender every event—every aspect of life. Holy Love does not insist on its own way (1 Corinthians Chap. 13), but asks for God's Divine Will to triumph in every situation. When you pray this small prayer,* **'God's Will be done'**, *the good angels align themselves against any evil that is affecting the present moment."*

Jesus
June 3, 2002

IN THE NAME OF JESUS

"Realize the power of My Name—indeed, the power of calling on your Jesus in times of temptation and trial. **When you say My Name**, *all of Heaven comes to attention. The power of My Precious Blood covers you and evil is made to vanish. When you say even more—*

Sacred Heart Ejaculation

Sacred Heart of Jesus, have mercy on us.

—*evil will be revealed, for Satan cannot remain hidden when I am thus invoked. When you pray*—

United Hearts Ejaculation

United Hearts of Jesus and
Mary, guide and protect us.

—*Satan not only flees but the path you must follow in righteousness is laid bare."*

Jesus
June 5, 2003

PRAYER OF LOVE AND THANKS

Jesus, I love You. Thank you.

*"My brothers and sisters, I desire that you show Me how much you love Me moment to moment by giving Me all the little chores, burdens and victories of the day. Simply say to Me as each moment comes and goes, '**Jesus, I love You. Thank you**.' I love you*

much in return. I hold sovereignty over all the present moments of your life."

Jesus
July 7, 2003

PRAYER POSTURE FOR PETITIONS

Jesus, You are my strength. Alone, I can do nothing. Only You can fulfill this petition.

"Tonight I desire that you understand the proper prayer posture interiorly to have when you pray for a petition. When you desire that a petition be answered, My brothers and sisters, cast the petition upon the altar of My Sacred Heart. Place all your faith and hope and trust in the goodness of My Sacred Heart. Say to me, 'Jesus, You are my strength. Alone, I can do nothing. Only You can fulfill this petition.' And then leave the petition in My Heart. Every time it comes to mind, surrender it again in this manner. This pleases Me."

Jesus
September 19, 2005

MARY AS PROTECTRESS AND REFUGE

Mary, Protectress of the Faith and Refuge of Holy Love.

112

"Now I come to you under a new title 'Refuge of Holy Love'. My faithful children have the power to carry this title into the world along with the title 'Protectress of the Faith'. Do so! When you repeat **'Mary, Protectress of the Faith and Refuge of Holy Love,'** *the enemy will flee. It will be your spiritual refuge in the troubles which lie ahead."*

Blessed Mother
November 25, 2002

KEY TO THE CHAMBER OF HOLY LOVE

*M*ary, Protectress of the Faith and Refuge of Holy Love, come to my aid.

"Today I have come to help you see that the most important step in personal holiness lies at the threshold of entry into the First Chamber—the Immaculate Heart of Mary—Holy Love. It is upon this threshold the soul is engaged in the greatest spiritual warfare. It is at the entrance of My Mother's Heart the soul decides to believe or disbelieve in these Messages."

*"Some souls lie permanently vanquished at the threshold, giving in to the pride of disbelief. Others see the spiritual benefit they are being offered. They pick up the key to the Chamber of Holy Love which is the title and ejaculatory prayer, '***Mary, Protectress of the***

Faith and Refuge of Holy Love, come to my aid.'
*Thus they are admitted and led deeper into the
Chambers of Our United Hearts. Pray for those who
arrive at the threshold."*

Jesus
February 10, 2006

Mary, Refuge of Holy Love

Chapter 10. *Novenas*

****

In This Chapter:

****

FIVE-DAY NOVENA TO
MARY, REFUGE OF HOLY LOVE

Dictated by St. Bernard of Clairvaux

February 8-24, 2008

"I have come so that the world will understand that the building blocks—the foundation of trust—are the virtues of faith, hope and love. The stronger these three virtues, the deeper the trust in God."

St. Bernard of Clairvaux
February 15, 2008

To be recited daily during the Novena:

PRAYER TO MARY, PROTECTRESS AND REFUGE

*M*ary, my Mother, Protectress and Refuge— Your Immaculate Heart is our safe harbor in any storm. Manifest now the power God has given You in answer to this plea—Mary, Protectress of the Faith and Refuge of Holy Love. Amen.

(February 8, 2008)

DAY ONE *(February 15, 2008)*

*S*weetest Mary, our Refuge and Protectress, increase within us the virtues of faith, hope and love so that our trust in You will be unfailing. Amen.

Prayer to Mary, Protectress and Refuge…

DAY TWO *(February 17, 2008)*

*D*earest Mary, You are our Protectress and Refuge. Hide me in the deepest recesses of Your Heart which is pure love. Protect me from the snares and temptations of Satan. Help me to conform to God's Divine Will in every present moment. Amen.

Prayer to Mary, Protectress and Refuge…

DAY THREE *(February 21, 2008)*

$\mathcal{M}$ary, my Mother, Protectress and Refuge, open the inner recesses of Your Heart to me. Purify my soul—poor sinner that I am—in the Flame of Your Heart.

I surrender to You now all my sins, that which leads me into sin, and all my lack of trust. Help me to conform to the Divine Will of God. Amen.

Prayer to Mary, Protectress and Refuge…

DAY FOUR *(February 22, 2008)*

$\mathcal{M}$ary, my Mother and Refuge, let the grace of Your Heart, which is Holy Love, pour into my soul just as sunlight splashes across the face of the earth.

Enlighten my heart as to the ways I can show Jesus I love Him more, and thus come deeper into personal holiness. Amen.

Prayer to Mary, Protectress and Refuge…

DAY FIVE *(February 24, 2008)*

$\mathcal{M}$ary, Refuge of Holy Love, as we complete this novena, be so kind as to extend to us the grace of the fulfillment of our petition according to the Eternal Father's Will. Then grant us the grace of accepting God's Divine Will as He manifests it. Amen.

Prayer to Mary, Protectress and Refuge…

NOVENA TO GOD THE FATHER

Dictated by Alanus (Angel)
July 31, 2007 – August 4, 2007

To be recited daily during the Novena:

PRAYER TO GOD THE FATHER

*H*eavenly Father, Eternal Now, Creator of the Universe, Splendor of Heaven, listen with compassion to Your children who cry out to You. Pour out upon the earth Your Provision, Your Mercy, Your Love. With the winnowing fan of Your Divine Will, separate good from evil.

Remove the cloud of deception Satan has placed over the heart of the world so that all people and every nation choose good over evil. No longer allow us to suffer from the evil choices of those who oppose Your Eternal Divine Will.

Dictated by Angels
July 30, 2007

DAY ONE *(July 31, 2007)*

*D*ear Heavenly Father, we pray that Your Divine Will, which is Holy Love, be made known to all people and all nations. Show those that embrace evil, violence and acts of terrorism that these things are never Your Will and do not please You, but offend You gravely. Amen.

Our Father – Hail Mary – All Glory Be –
Prayer to God the Father

DAY TWO *(July 31, 2007)*

*H*eavenly Father, Splendor of Truth, help me always to trust in Your Divine Will, which is One with Your Provision, Your Mercy and Your Love. Through Your Divine Will, assist me in always living in the truth. Amen.

Our Father – Hail Mary – All Glory Be –
Prayer to God the Father

DAY THREE *(August 2, 2007)*

*A*bba Father! You are the Eternal Now, the Creator of time and space, the Source of all that is good. In every present moment, I beseech You, help me to find Your Divine Will and to surrender to It. Amen.

Our Father – Hail Mary – All Glory Be –
Prayer to God the Father

DAY FOUR *(August 2, 2007)*

*E*ternal Father, allow Your Divine Will to mold my heart in every virtue, to shape my spirituality according to Holy and Divine Love. Thus may it please You to make me an instrument of Your Will in the world. Amen."

*Our Father – Hail Mary – All Glory Be –
Prayer to God the Father*

DAY FIVE *(August 3, 2007)*

*H*eavenly Father, All Powerful and All Knowing God, Ever Present in the tabernacles of the world, grant the heart of the world the grace to recognize Your Will in the world today, which is always love and truth. Amen.

*Our Father – Hail Mary – All Glory Be –
Prayer to God the Father*

DAY SIX *(August 3, 2007)*

*E*ternal Father, in Your Omniscience, You understand that Divine Love is engaged in the final battle against hate that Satan sows in hearts. Help us to be Your weapons of victory over every evil that opposes Your Divine Will, which is always Divine Love. Amen.

*Our Father – Hail Mary – All Glory Be –
Prayer to God the Father*

DAY SEVEN *(August 3, 2007)*

*H*eavenly Father, Source of All Grace, You created us in Your Image. Help us always to be reflections of Your Heart, which is Paternal Divine Love in the world. Amen.

Our Father – Hail Mary – All Glory Be –
Prayer to God the Father

DAY EIGHT *(August 4, 2007)*

*H*eavenly Father, Creator of the Universe, place in our hearts today the will to live in harmony with Your Holy and Divine Will. We know this is only possible through Holy and Divine Love. Help us to choose this Love in every present moment. Amen.

Our Father – Hail Mary – All Glory Be –
Prayer to God the Father

DAY NINE *(August 4, 2007)*

*E*ternal Father and my Father, Your Mercy and Love fill all the earth. Reach into every heart and reclaim each one as Your Own through the light of truth and righteousness. If it is Your Divine Will, grant me, Your needy child, this petition I invoke of You *(name petition)*. Amen.

Our Father – Hail Mary – All Glory Be –
Prayer to God the Father

PART TWO: PRAYERS AND DEVOTIONS

Chapter 11. *Divine Victimhood Prayers*

****

In This Chapter:

Victimhood of Love Prayer
Surrender of Heart to Victimhood of Love
The Call to Divine Victimhood

****

VICTIMHOOD OF LOVE PRAYER

Dear Jesus, in this present moment, for love of You, I accept the cross no matter what form it takes. I desire to heal Your wounded Heart through this Victimhood of Love. Amen.

"Each day and in every present moment, the cross takes on a new form in every person's life. Be ready by accepting the cross for love of Me. This is the way of Divine Victimhood—the way to become a Victim of Love. In your acceptance is your surrender."

"When you arise, pray thus."

"Repeat this prayer throughout the day or whenever the cross presents itself in a difficult way."

Jesus
August 31, 2006

SURRENDER OF HEART TO VICTIMHOOD OF LOVE

Dear Sacred Heart of Jesus and Sorrowing Heart of Mary, I give You my whole heart, every joy and sorrow, every iniquity and all merit that You find in it today. I offer to You my desire to be Your victim of love. With this desire, see my trust in Your Will for me, and allow this trust to console You. Amen.

Jesus
April 18, 2003 / Good Friday – 3:00 p.m.

THE CALL TO DIVINE VICTIMHOOD

"I am your Jesus, born Incarnate. Alleluia!"

"Today I have come to describe to you this beautiful treasure which I esteem more than any other in a soul who embraces it. It is Divine Victimhood. Such a soul gives to Me everything—great and small, joy and trial alike—towards the conversion of sinners. Though their sacrifices remain hidden from the world, I tabulate everything in My Heart and measure it according to the love with which it is offered."

"Divine victims carry the weight of error on their shoulders with joy, for they know they are assisting Me just as I carried My Cross. Their sacrifices reach through time into eternity."

"I call all who will listen—to respond to Divine Victimhood with courage, with love."

(March 29, 2005)

"I am your Jesus, born Incarnate. Alleluia!"

"I am here to explain to you the meaning behind the symbol I showed you yesterday."

"First of all, My Body is not on the Cross. You must mount the Cross for Me with love. The Flames of Holy and Divine Love are on the Cross to remind you to sacrifice everything with love. The little flame represents the Holy and Divine Love in your heart which must be on the Cross to bring Me souls."

"Render Me the kindness of reproducing this image so that souls may wear it as a reminder of My call to Divine Victimhood."

(The Flame of Divine Love is the largest;
Next in size is the Flame of Holy Love;
Smallest is the flame of the victim soul.)
(March 30, 2005)

Chapter 12. *Offering Of Past Crosses*

****

In This Chapter:

Offering of Past Crosses

****

OFFERING OF PAST CROSSES

Jesus and Blessed Mother are here with Their Hearts exposed. They nod Their Heads, greeting everyone here in the room. Blessed Mother says: "Praise be to Jesus." Jesus says: "I am your Jesus, born Incarnate."

Jesus: "Today, as always, I come to speak to My Remnant Faithful. The heart of the world is in turmoil, spurned and fed by aggressive self-love. I need My army of victim souls—those who choose Divine Victimhood with loving hearts—to appease My Most Wounded Heart in this hour of distress, which weighs the world down in sin and error."

"So, today, the Father wills I come to you with this important revelation. While it is true that once past, the present moment is gone forever; it is also true that all humanity lives in the Eternal Now, for there is no time or space in eternity. Therefore, living in the present in the Eternal Now, you can give to Me all that you suffered in the past as redemptive grace for souls who travel the road to perdition. There are just two conditions. You must have been in a state of grace when you suffered the particular cross you now desire to give Me, and you must have suffered it with love."

"This means every insult, every illness—even as an infant, if you were baptized at the time—every inconvenience, every embarrassment can now be given to Me as a gift! This increases and strengthens the arsenal of weapons I will use against evil in the world. All you need do is say:

Offering of Past Crosses

Jesus, I give to You with love,
all my past crosses.

Then I will take even the smallest crosses, even the ones you do not remember, and use them to save souls. It is a great victory in the war against evil that I am able to tell you this today."

"There are certain conditions which weaken your offering to Me of past crosses. One would be if the soul is not in a state of grace at the moment he offers to Me all past suffering. Another would be if he is assailed with doubts about the Message itself. But even these conditions which weaken the offering will not negate completely the total act of consecrating past crosses to Me. Instead, I will inspire the soul to be properly disposed, and to offer these past crosses to Me again."

"You must understand what a great grace this is that I give to the world today. [He has a quiver of arrows over His Shoulder, and it seems the tips are flames.] With this arsenal I can reach the hearts of errant leaders and weaken their aggressive nature. You who offer Me these past crosses are helping Me to close the abyss between Heaven and earth, and to restore harmony between the Eternal Divine Will of My Father and man's free will."

"The only thing you lose forever in the present moment is that which is not loving. The only thing which you save in the Eternal Now is all that you think, say and do in Holy Love. Holy and Divine Love are eternal."

"As more and more souls relinquish to Me all their past crosses—great and small—I am opening wide the First Chamber of Our United Hearts, the Heart of My Mother, which is Holy Love."

"As more and more souls turn to Me by merit of the powerful force of this offering of past crosses, Satan's attacks upon this Mission of Our United Hearts will be more easily discerned and readily thwarted. Therefore, understand that the more who offer to Me their past crosses in this way, the weaker Satan becomes. It is necessary that you comprehend this and with dispatch, propagate this Message. Many souls, many vocations, many marriages will be saved in this way."

"The power of these sacrifices of past crosses from souls around the world will allow Me to stop wars, reveal evil that is nurtured under the cover of darkness, strengthen the Remnant and the Tradition of Faith, and calm erratic forces of nature. Perhaps, then, you see the significance of My words to you today."

"My brothers and sisters, please understand that when you atone to the Hearts of Jesus and Mary, you also appease the Heart of the Divine Father. Thus, by offering Me the crosses in your past life, the circle is complete; the Hour of Mercy extends, and My Justice is delayed by the Will of God."

Jesus extends His Hands out over the people and says: "Today We're extending to you the Blessing of Our United Hearts."

(November 5, 2006 / Monthly Message to
All People and Every Nation)

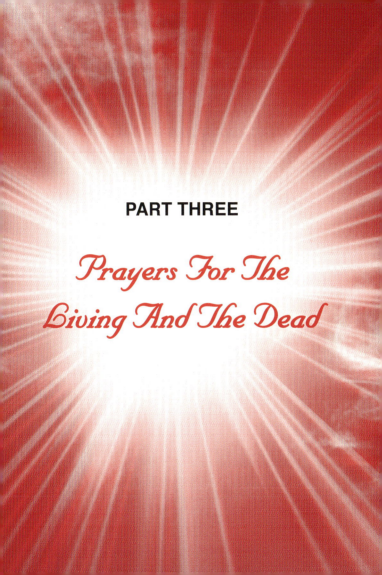

PART THREE

*Prayers For The
Living And The Dead*

Chapter 13. *Prayers For The World*

* *

In This Chapter:

* *

MISSIONARY PRAYER

"I am moved by the many prayers offered here to give to the world the following prayer, which, if propagated and accepted by all people and every nation, will change the course of human events."

133

I choose with my free will to love God above all else, and my neighbor as myself. I choose this—Holy Love in the present moment—and seek God's help in doing so in every future moment. Amen.

Jesus' September 5, 2005 Monthly Message to
All People and Every Nation

ECUMENICAL PRAYER FOR PEACE

Heavenly Father, turn Your benevolent gaze towards us. Place all people—all nations—in your Paternal Embrace. Inspire every heart to live according to Holy Love, for this is the way of true peace. Amen.

Dictated by an Angel
December 26, 2003

PRAYER OF PETITION TO LIVE IN
THE DIVINE WILL

Heavenly Father, during this time of world crisis, let all souls find their peace and security in Your Divine Will. Give each soul the grace to understand that Your Will is Holy Love in the present moment.

Benevolent Father, illuminate each conscience to see the ways that he is not living in Your Will. Grant the world the grace to change and the time in which to do it. Amen.

"My daughter, when you pray for peace, let your prayer be one for conversion of hearts. Do not forget, as you pray, that the terrorists are My children, as well. They, more than any, need a conviction of conscience which leads to conversion."

"Ask your country to pray this prayer. Begin with My Missionary Servants of Holy Love..."

"This prayer should be recited at the beginning of the Rosary and before the Creed. Besides that, it needs to be propagated far and wide. I charge My Missionary Servants of Holy Love with this task."

Mary, Mother of God
September 28, 2001
(After the 9/11 Terrorist Attack on the USA)

PRAYER TO GOD THE FATHER

*H*eavenly Father, Eternal Now, Creator of the Universe, Splendor of Heaven, listen with compassion to Your children who cry out to You. Pour out upon the earth Your Provision, Your Mercy, Your Love. With the winnowing fan of Your Divine Will, separate good from evil.

Remove the cloud of deception Satan has placed over the heart of the world so that all people and every nation choose good over evil. No longer allow us to suffer from the evil choices of those who oppose Your Eternal Divine Will.

"This is a prayer the Heavenly Father will listen closely to, as consciences these days oppose good and promote evil."

Dictated by Angels
July 30, 2007

CONSECRATION OF NATIONS TO GOD'S DIVINE WILL

I, (*Name*), as leader of this nation of _____, desire to consecrate this country to God's Divine Will which is Love and Mercy itself. I realize that the future of this nation depends upon Divine Mercy and Divine Love.

I resolve to avoid offending God's Will in any way through supporting legislation which is contrary to His Love and Mercy, or in taking any diplomatic measure which transgresses human rights. I surrender the future to God's Will and His Provision. Amen.

"I have come so that the leaders of every nation can put this prayer to use."

Jesus
May 29, 2006

CONSECRATION OF THE WORLD TO THE UNITED HEARTS

(Please see Chapter 14)

PRAYER FOR UNITY AND PEACE AMONGST ALL PEOPLE AND ALL NATIONS

*H*eavenly Father, we come to Your Paternal Heart seeking peace amongst all people and all nations. Bring into harmony with Your Divine Will all human life, all of nature—even the cosmos itself.

"Protect all of creation from Satan's destructive plans. We know that war must be in hearts before it is in the world. Inspire all mankind, dear Father, to choose love of God and neighbor, which leads to true peace, for we know this is Your Will for us. Amen."

St. Thomas Aquinas
July 23, 2006

Jesus: "Today I invite all people and every nation to realize that abortion, war, famine and many more things are the bad fruit of inordinate self-love. Pray then, that all hearts be open to humility and self-effacement, for the future of the world lies at stake."

(July 23, 2006)

PRAYER TO OVERCOME HATRED IN HEARTS

*D*ear Sorrowing Sacred Heart of Jesus, humbly we ask an infusion of grace upon the heart of the world. Sacred Chamber of Divine Love, redirect free will to choose Holy Love over hate. Listen to the plight of all mankind and help us to avoid war, terrorism and crimes against life."

Make us Your emissaries of Divine Love. Amen.

Jesus
March 7, 2003

PRAYER TO OVERCOME UNFORGIVENESS

Jesus, I trust in You. I know that You love me. I desire every obstacle between us be removed. Take from my heart any morsel of unforgiveness so that I can be completely Yours.

Help me to forgive those who have hurt me, have lied about me, have gossiped about me, were jealous of me, have stolen from me or have abused me in any way. Then plunge me deep into Your Most Sacred Heart. Cover Me with Your Most Precious Blood.

Do not allow me to resist Your Love again through unforgiveness of another. Amen.

"The Lord of Hosts says whole nations could benefit from this prayer."

Alanus (One of Maureen's Angels)
March 6, 2008

PRAYER PETITIONS

FOR THE WORLD TO
TO LIVE IN HOLY AND DIVINE LOVE

Jesus: "Today, My brothers and sisters, I am asking My Eternal Father and your Eternal Father to send the Spirit of TRUTH—THE HOLY SPIRIT out upon every nation and all people, inspiring them to live in Holy and Divine Love. Pray, My brothers and sisters, that hearts follow this inspiration, for it is the way to true peace."

(May 27, 2007 / Feast of Pentecost)

FOR RUSSIA, CHINA AND THE ARAB NATIONS

Jesus: "My Mother asks especially prayers for China—next, She asks for prayers for Russia and for the Arab Nations. Peace is very, very fragile in the Arab Nations. These Messages are for all people and all nations. Do not keep them to yourselves."

(December 12, 2004)

THAT ALL LEADERS ABANDON THE FALSE
CONSCIENCE AND RETURN TO THE SECURE
PATH OF TRUTH

St. Thomas Aquinas: "If you look at the heart of the world today, you could say that most of the choices made that affect the whole world arise from a false sense of right and wrong. Governments choose abortion over life, war over peace, unequal distribution of world goods, resulting in starvation for some. Right reason has taken flight on many such issues, and the father of lies continues to influence judgment."

"Pray that all leaders return to the secure path of truth, and abandon the false conscience that contradicts life itself and the Will of God. I will pray with you."

(August 30, 2007)

FOR THE UNCONVERTED

Blessed Mother: "My dear, dear children, when you pray, pray for all the unconverted and cover your prayers with the Most Precious Blood of My Beloved Son, Jesus. Satan is strong today. He knows he is engaged in a desperate battle. You must be ready and prepared. Pray for all My children who believe that they walk the path of righteousness, but who are deceived."

(June 19, 2003)

FOR THE CYNICAL HEARTS OF UNBELIEVERS

Jesus: "My brothers and sisters, it is important that you realize that the heart of the world has embraced cynicism to such a degree that it is impossible for many to accept the truths of the Messages of Holy and Divine Love. This same spirit prevents them from seeing the errors in their own hearts. Therefore, I continue, and repeat asking you to pray for unbelievers."

(December 17, 2007)

TO CONSTRUCT A BRIDGE OF HOLY AND DIVINE LOVE BETWEEN HEAVEN AND EARTH

Jesus: "My brothers and sisters, the reason for My visits to this site are to reconcile mankind with his Creator through Holy Love, and lead all into the Chambers of Our United Hearts. So much do I desire that a bridge of Holy and Divine Love be constructed through prayer and sacrifice between Heaven and earth. Pray for this."

(March 4, 2005)

FOR FREE WILL TO BE RECONCILED WITH THE FATHER'S DIVINE WILL

Jesus: "My brothers and sisters, tonight I desire very much to spread over the entire earth a blanket of Holy and Divine Love; thus, the heart of the world would be warmed and reconciled with My Father and His Divine Will. But it is free will that prevents Me from accomplishing this—free will which I always respect. Therefore, My brothers and sisters, you must pray that free will is reconciled with the Divine Will of My Father."

(December 7, 2007)

TO UNCOVER THE ENEMY'S LIES AND CONVERT UNBELIEVERS

Mary, Refuge of Holy Love: "Dear little children, I come to you once again to draw all people and all nations into My Immaculate Heart, and so too, into the Eucharistic Heart of My Jesus. At the appointed time, chosen and known only by the Eternal Father, all people will be given the grace to know and to understand His Real Presence. Many will be drawn into His Heart by means of this forthcoming miracle. But you must pray, My children. Prayer unites you to God and helps you to recognize evil. The ones who are most in need of this miracle will be the ones most likely to reject it. Turn your hearts into a living oblation in imitation of the Eucharistic Heart. In this way unbelievers will be given more graces towards their conversion."

"…The Arm of My Son's Justice grows heavy. I need your help—your prayers—to hold it back.

(June 24, 2006 / Midnight Service)

FOR JESUS' VICTORY TO COME INTO EVERY HEART SOON

Jesus: "Today, My brothers and sisters, I once again call all nations to be united in the truth—the truth of the Cross—the truth of Holy and Divine Love. My Mother sorrows for those who do not live according to the truth, but She weeps for those who know the truth but disregard it. Pray for My victory to come into every heart soon."

(July 22, 2007)

TO OVERCOME THE NETWORK OF EVIL IN THE WORLD

Jesus: "There is a network of evil in the world which is choking out the honest and good, and calling to the forefront, evil control. It is only through prayer and fasting that these certain and diabolic organizations will crumble and no longer promote their hidden agendas. Therefore, I say once again, the future of the world rests in the hands of the Remnant Faithful."

(June 17, 2007 / Midnight Service)

When You Pray For Others

Jesus: "I will deny you nothing that is a reasonable need. When you ask for something for the welfare of others, it is already yours. Such a petition has been in My Heart since the beginning of time. It does not languish in My Heart, but bears good fruit in the world."

(April 7, 2008)

MESSAGES FROM GOD THE FATHER

"I am God the Father, Creator of Heaven and earth. I reign over all creatures. My Kingdom is in every heart who does My Will. I have created the saint and sinner alike. It is free will that separates good from evil. It is free will which determines the future of each soul and the future of the world."

"I ask the world to hear and understand in their heart that no war effort, no negotiation, no leader can bring peace and security into the world unless My Divine Will is the block you build it upon."

"My Divine Will is Holy Love."

(September 28, 2001)

Once again I see a great Flame around the tabernacle. I hear a voice say: "I am the Eternal Now, the Eternal Father. I am not a rock or a crystal or a tree. I am the Creator of all that exists in time and space. I call each of you to your salvation through the Chambers of the United Hearts, which is a transforming love."

"I do not encourage violence—not in the womb—not within your hearts—not within the context of any so-called religion, for I am Unity and Peace. Pray for a worldwide realization of the truth that I have put forth here today."

(February 19, 2008)

Chapter 14. *Worldwide Consecration To The United Hearts*

****

In This Chapter:

Consecration of the World to the United Hearts
About the Worldwide Consecration to the United Hearts

****

CONSECRATION OF THE WORLD TO THE UNITED HEARTS
(To be recited by Church Leaders)

*H*eavenly Father, in this present moment, which You have created and willed, I _____ *(name)* _____, do hereby consecrate the heart of this country, _____ *(name)* _____ to the United Hearts of the Holy Trinity in union with the Immaculate Heart of Mary.

Dictated by God the Father
September 18, 2007

ABOUT THE WORLDWIDE CONSECRATION TO THE UNITED HEARTS

Jesus and Blessed Mother are here with Their Hearts exposed. Blessed Mother says: "Praise be to Jesus." Jesus says: "I am your Jesus, born Incarnate."

Jesus: "The way to world peace is only through Holy and Divine Love. Therefore, I am seeking this worldwide consecration to Our United Hearts so that the heart of the world can be affected towards the change for good. This way the grace will be given to all political leaders to see their errors and their sins against love. I am counting on My Church leaders—all Church leaders, all ecclesiasticals—to carry out My requests."

"I am aware of the petitions in hearts of the needs that every soul has. Listen and watch for God's Holy and Divine Will in your lives."

"We're blessing you with the Complete Blessing of Our United Hearts."

(September 15, 2007 / Feast of the Sorrowful Mother – 3:00 p.m. Service in the United Hearts Field)

Jesus and Blessed Mother are here with Their Hearts exposed. Blessed Mother says: "Praise be to Jesus." Jesus says: "I am your Jesus, born Incarnate."

Jesus: "My brothers and sisters, we have shared the time together this weekend. Carry the devotion to Our United Hearts back to your points of origin. I plead with you—follow through in having your nations consecrated to Our United Hearts, for it is in this way that the heart of the world will be transformed into a heart of Holy and Divine Love. It is in this way that each political figure will understand what he must do in righteousness." [A personal message was given.]

Jesus: "We're extending to you the Complete Blessing of Our United Hearts."

During the fifth mystery of the rosary, Alanus was here. * He said: "Praise be to Jesus."

"The world can only find peace through the United Hearts of Jesus and Mary. Pray and sacrifice that Holy and Divine Love grip the heart of the world. Pray and sacrifice."

(September 17, 2007)

Alanus is one of Maureen's angels.

I (Maureen) see a great Flame that I have come to know as the Heart of God the Father, and then I hear:

"I am the Eternal Father—the Eternal Now."

"Before time began—before I created time and space—I knew you. I knew what you would be doing in this present moment. I knew the sins you fell into. I know your weaknesses now. I love you."

"The Message given on the Feast of Sorrows proceeds from a troubled Heart of your Father. It is given as a last alternative to Divine Justice in the face of the multitude of sin and error throughout the world."

"If all nations will listen—if Church leaders throughout the world will adhere to My wishes—the

147

heart of the world will turn white with innocence once again. World leaders will be shown their mistakes and convicted of their errors. I even give you, O man, the leniency, that this consecration does not need to be coordinated into a specific time frame. Rather, when you hear My Voice through this Message, accomplish My request. This is My Divine Will. I speak to all churches—all governments—all ecclesiastics. Speak up thus for righteousness:"

[God the Father then gives church leaders the consecration prayer]

"If enough accomplish this and answer My request, you will gradually see governments change their policies, and finally, the heart of the world will return to innocence."

(September 18, 2007)

Jesus is here with His Heart exposed. He has a brilliant white light around Him, and there is a great Flame around the white light. It looks like the Father's Paternal Heart that I have come to know recently. Jesus says: "I am your Jesus, born Incarnate."

Jesus: "Today I have come to reiterate the need for the heart of the world to be consecrated to Our United Hearts. All that opposes this is outside the Will of My Father. This consecration of individual countries will serve as a sin offering and a protection from Satan's attacks. It is the Merciful Hand of My Father that offers this grace in the midst of chaos and confusion."

"You must see that I cannot shepherd you away from sin if your hearts carry you elsewhere. This consecration of whole countries, of churches and congregations will renew in hearts the goal of personal holiness—a goal that holds little value in the world today."

"Through the Father's Will, I desire that the world be transformed into a new creation—a creation of Holy and Divine Love. You have the technology to make Heaven's plan known; if you hear Me, put it to use."

"While the world waits and watches for the next act of terrorism, the next natural disaster, I invite you to believe in the solution Heaven has given you. Do not waste time in contemplating ways this plan might fail. Face the grave reality of the place the world is in today and decide to help Me; decide to help all of humanity."

"Holy and Divine Love are never wrong. Therefore, the Vessels of Holy and Divine Love—the United Hearts—must be regarded as trustworthy in Their Essence and Their Call to Humanity. To choose Holy and Divine Love is to choose the Heart of the Father and, therefore, His Mighty Divine Will."

"Do not adopt the spirit of the world as your own— the spirit that encourages gloom and doom—the spirit that discourages the solution Heaven offers, and prefers to await the Hand of Justice. I do not desire to impart My Justice upon the world. Rather, I invite the heart of the world into My Heart of Mercy and Love. Heed My call! Accept My invitation with gratitude."

"My Father, Who is the Creator of all good, offers the grace of this consecration as a means of being once more united to all mankind as was His Will from the beginning of time. The consecration would form a bridge between Heaven and earth—a bridge between man's free will and His Divine Will. It would be a bridge of love."

"My dear brothers and sisters, do all you can to further this consecration in hearts and in the world. For I tell you, it is when this bridge is constructed by merit of this consecration, the Cross and the Victory will become one again."

"Today I'm extending to you the Complete Blessing of Our United Hearts."

> (October 5, 2007 / Monthly Message to
> All People and Every Nation)

Jesus: "I desire to fill the world with My Merciful Love. This alone is the reason I speak here. Once again I ask for the consecration of the world to the United Hearts of the Most Blessed Trinity and the Immaculate Heart of Mary. Then I will triumph and reign!"

> (March 5, 2008 / Monthly Message to
> All People and Every Nation)

Chapter 15. *The Rosary Of The Unborn*

✳✳

In This Chapter:

Prayer to Be Recited with the Rosary of the Unborn
Vision of the Rosary of the Unborn
Use and Propagate the Rosary of the Unborn
The Impact of One Abortion

✳✳

PRAYER TO BE RECITED WITH THE ROSARY OF THE UNBORN

Divine Infant Jesus, as we pray this rosary, we ask you to remove from the heart of the world the desire to commit the sin of abortion. Remove the veil of deceit Satan has placed over hearts which portrays promiscuity as a freedom, and reveal it for what it is— slavery to sin.

Place over the heart of the world a renewed respect for life at the moment of conception. Amen.

Blessed Mother
August 27, 2005

VISION OF THE ROSARY OF THE UNBORN

Our Lady comes in white. In front of Her and suspended in the air is an unusual rosary. The Our Father beads are droplets of blood in the shape of a cross. The Hail Mary beads are light blue tear drops with unborn babies inside of them. The cross is gleaming gold. Our Lady says: "I come in praise of Jesus, My Son. I come as Prophetess of these times."

"The rosary you see is Heaven's way of describing to you the weapon that will overcome this evil of abortion. Heaven weeps for the cost of this great sin. The history and the future of all nations has been changed because of this atrocity against God's gift of life."

"Today, sadly, much responsibility must be placed on the laity who are consecrated to Me. I cannot depend on Church leadership to unite in an effort to vanquish the enemy through the Rosary. Even My apparitions have caused division by Satan's efforts to thwart My plans."

"So today, on My feast day, I am calling all My children to unite in My Heart. Do not allow pride to divide you according to which apparition you will follow. Become part of the Flame of My Heart. Be united in love and in the prayer weapon of My Rosary. The evil of abortion can be conquered by your efforts and through My grace."

"Propagate the image I have shown you today."

(October 7, 1997 / Feast of the Holy Rosary)

Promises Attendant to the Rosary

1. "I affirm to you, my daughter, that **each 'Hail Mary' prayed from a loving heart will rescue one of these innocent lives from death by abortion.** When you use this rosary, call to mind My Sorrowful Immaculate Heart which continually sees the sin of abortion played out in every present moment. I give to you this special sacramental* with which to heal My Motherly Heart."

    Maureen asks: "Blessed Mother, do you mean any 'Hail Mary' or just one prayed on the Rosary of the Unborn?"

    Blessed Mother: "This is a special grace attached to this particular rosary. It should always be used to pray against abortion. You will please make this known."

    *Note: In order to be a sacramental, it must be blessed by a Catholic Priest.

    Our Lady as the Sorrowful Mother
July 2, 2001

2. "Please tell the world that **each 'Our Father' recited on the Rosary of the Unborn assuages My grieving Heart. Further, it withholds the Arm of Justice.**"

    Jesus
August 3, 2001

3.   "The greatest promise I give you in regards to this rosary is this: **Every Rosary prayed from the heart to its completion on these beads mitigates the punishment as yet withstanding for the sin of abortion.**"

"…When I say the punishment as yet withstanding for the sin of abortion, I mean the punishment each soul deserves for taking part in this sin. Then too, I also refer to the greater punishment that awaits the world for embracing this sin."

Jesus
August 3, 2001

4.   If a group is gathered who are praying for the unborn from the heart and only one person has in their possession the Rosary of the Unborn, **I will honor each 'Hail Mary' from each person in the group** as if they were holding the Rosary of the Unborn themselves."

"In this way I lift the constraint of time which it takes to produce enough rosaries."

Jesus
February 28, 2005

USE AND PROPAGATE THE ROSARY OF THE UNBORN

Blessed Mother says: "Praise be to Jesus."

"My Son allows Me to come here today as I did so many years ago in Lourdes. Today, I invite the world to pray the Rosary of the Unborn and to propagate it with the promises. I give it now, as My Son prescribes, not for anyone's material gain but to stop the terrible sin of abortion. You do not realize how many ways you are hurting yourselves by rejecting life in the womb. In every present moment, a life is snuffed out."

"When you use this rosary, you save lives with each 'Hail Mary'. You hold My Teardrops in your fingers, which envelope every life that is threatened. Embrace this sacramental, dear children, just as you embrace life itself."

(February 11, 2008 / Feast of Our Lady of Lourdes)

Pray By The Manger For All Life To Be Respected

Jesus: "My brothers and sisters, during this joyous time of year, I desire even more to renew the face of the earth and to bring each soul to the realization that all life from natural conception to natural death must be respected. Therefore, I invite every soul to kneel by the manger and ask My Tiny Sacred Heart to flood the world with the grace it needs towards this intention."

(December 9, 2007)

THE IMPACT OF ONE ABORTION

Jesus: "Today I come to help society understand the impact of just one abortion upon the world. When human life, which is divinely created in the womb is destroyed by the sin of abortion, the course of human history is changed forever. All which that human being would have accomplished in his lifetime is left abandoned. In place of this life given by Heaven, Satan is allowed to place an angel of darkness, which influences all the lives that would have been touched by the one sacrificed upon the altar of abortion—the altar of self-love."

"This is the reason for so much evil in the world today. You are living in a world profoundly affected by this one sin alone—abortion."

(September 9, 2007)

✳✳

In This Chapter:

Children's Consecration to the United Hearts
Prayer to the Divine Child Jesus to Protect
    Innocence

✳✳

CHILDREN'S CONSECRATION
TO THE UNITED HEARTS

Dear United Hearts of Jesus and Mary, I love You very much. I want to give You this present moment and all the future moments of my life. I always want to please You. I give You my heart today and always, and pray You will unite it to Your United Hearts.

Place in my heart, dear Jesus and Mary, the desire to help sinners turn to You. Amen.

"Copy this prayer to the United Hearts. It can serve as a consecration of children to the Two Hearts. Propagate it among the young."

St. Margaret Mary Alacoque
October 12, 2006

PRAYER TO THE DIVINE CHILD JESUS TO PROTECT INNOCENCE

Divine Child Jesus, we come to You asking Your protection over the innocence of the world. Place all children in Your little Divine Heart.

Protect their eyes so that they do not see anything that would destroy their innocence. Protect their ears that they would not hear anything that would take away innocence. Fill their hearts with Holy Love, dear Divine Child. Extend their years of innocence by merit of Your protection. Amen.

"I have come to give to the world a prayer to protect the innocence of the world at large. Satan has made it his goal to destroy innocence at an early age, thus claiming more and more souls for himself. The prayer is to My Image of Divine Childhood."

Jesus
October 9, 2006

Jesus: "Today, the innocence of childhood is violated like unripened fruit plucked from a tree and consumed by the voracious appetite of sin. Innocence is no longer cherished or safeguarded, but has become the victim of sinful appetites. This is what forms deep in the heart of souls and whole nations. It is a call for My Justice."

(July 5, 2004 / Monthly Message to
All People and Every Nation)

Chapter 17. Family Consecration To The United Hearts

****

In This Chapter:

Family Consecration Ceremony

****

St. Thomas Aquinas comes. He bows and prays before the tabernacle. He says: "Praise be to Jesus." He sits...

"You know the times are perilous. There is much speculation about the future. People live in fear, not trust. It is time for families to be consecrated to the United Hearts and to make a personal consecration to The Flame of Holy Love. This will be like the lamb's blood on the portal of their hearts and homes. Evil will pass over them and by them..."

October 31, 2001

FAMILY CONSECRATION CEREMONY

1. Gather your family.
2. Read the two Scripture passages.
3. Recite the three prayers given.
4. Display pictures of the United Hearts and of Mary, Refuge of Holy Love, in your home.
5. Pray the family consecration prayers on a daily basis. *(optional)*

2 Chronicles—Chapter 7, vs. 16

For now I have chosen and consecrated this house so that My Name may be there forever; My Eyes and My Heart will be there for all time.

Exodus—Chapter 12, vs. 7 and vs.13

Then they shall take some of the blood and put it on the two doorposts and the lintel of the houses in which they eat them. The blood shall be a sign for you, upon the houses where you are; and when I see the blood, I will pass over you, and no plague shall fall upon you to destroy you when I smite the land of Egypt.

Consecration to the Flame of Holy Love

*I*mmaculate Heart of Mary, humbly, I ask that You take my heart into the Flame of Holy Love, that is the Spiritual Refuge of all mankind. Do not look upon my faults and failings, but allow these iniquities to be burned away by this purifying Flame.

Through Holy Love, help me to be sanctified in the present moment, and in so doing, give to You, dear Mother, my every thought, word, and action. Take me and use me according to Your great pleasure. Allow me to be Your instrument in the world, all for the greater glory of God and towards Your victorious reign. Amen.

Dedication of Homes to Mary, Refuge of Holy Love

*M*ary, my Mother, my Fortress—Refuge of Holy Love—sanctify this home through Holy Love. Open each heart that dwells herein to holiness. Lead us along the path of Holy Love. Be victorious over any evil, whether it be an unknown force within these walls, a seductive habit, or some voluntary attachment we have chosen ourselves. Make this home a sanctuary of Holy Love. Amen.

Consecration of Families to
The United Hearts of Jesus and Mary

Sacred and United Hearts of Jesus and Mary, You are one in purpose as You desire the salvation, holiness, and sanctity of each soul. We consecrate our family to You seeking Your victory both in our hearts and in the world. We acknowledge the perfection of Your mercy in the past, the abundance of Your provision in the future, and the supreme sovereignty of the Father's Divine Will in this present moment. We desire to be part of Your triumphant reign beginning in this present moment through our 'yes' to Holy and Divine Love. We wish, with the help of Your grace, to live out this consecration through every future moment. Thus we will be united in triumph with You, dear United Hearts of Jesus and Mary. Amen.

Chapter 18. *Prayers For The Poor Souls In Purgatory*

* *

In This Chapter:

* *

VENERATION OF THE FIVE WOUNDS OF CHRIST

Say 5 times, once for each wound:

My Jesus, I love and venerate Your Sacred Wounds by whose merit I am redeemed.

"Teach My people to venerate My wounds in this manner. I promise each time this prayer is recited, a drop of My Precious Blood will fall on a soul suffering the flames of Purgatory."

Jesus

THE BLESSING OF PATERNAL LOVE

I extend the Blessing of Paternal Love to the Poor Souls in Purgatory.

"The Blessing of Paternal Love assists the soul in carrying his cross and mitigates Divine Justice through the cross. Thus, you should pass this Blessing on to the Poor Souls in Purgatory."

God the Father
July 24, 2007

PRAYER TO THE HOLY SOULS IN PURGATORY ON BEHALF OF THE CONFRATERNITY

(Please see Chapter 23)

"The Holy Souls in Purgatory are able to unite in prayer for certain causes."

Jesus
May 31, 2007

HOLY HOURS

Jesus: "When you make a holy hour and then recite an Our Father, Hail Mary and All Glory Be for the intentions of the Holy Father, the punishment due your sins is remitted. Or, if you offer these same prayers, but give the graces earned to a poor soul in Purgatory, he will be released."

(December 30, 2002)

ACTS OF REPARATION

Jesus: "I have come especially to ask you to pray and make acts of reparation. Do this especially to and for the Poor Souls in Purgatory, for these are the souls that pass into the Fifth Chamber of Our United Hearts."

(August 5, 2002 / Monthly Message to All Nations)

REFLECTION ON PURGATORY
By Alanus

Alanus (one of Maureen's angels) comes to me. He says: "All praise be to Jesus."

"Today in your country the citizens commemorate the dead by visiting cemeteries and decorating grave sites with flags, flowers and so forth. But what I have come to show you should change the outlook of all people concerning the hereafter if they enter into this vision of Purgatory with sincere hearts."

He then leads me, mystically, along a path which seems to be covered in brambles. We go up a little incline and he asks me to stand beside him on the edge of a rocky cliff. He motions with a sweep of his arm, and below us is a big canyon. At one end are great flames. It looks like people in silhouettes bobbing up and down in these flames. There are loud cries for mercy and shouts of pain, but it does not alleviate the suffering.

Alanus says, "**These are the souls in greatest need of prayer and sacrifice.** This is the lowest part of Purgatory—the part closest to Hell itself. Many suffer here, for no one prays for them. They were regarded as 'good'—some even 'holy'—in their lifetime, but it was all a façade. Many priests are among these poor souls, for they were not faithful to the precepts of the Church."

"There are those who lied about others, and destroyed their reputations. These are them." He shows me souls who are having molten lead poured down their throats. It burns holes through their necks but does not stop. On a ledge around this fire are many angels—more than I can count. Alanus says, "These are the guardian angels of those poor souls being purified at this level. Through all of this suffering, the souls' greatest trial is separation from God."

I saw souls who seemed to have their flesh melting away. This, too, was unending. Alanus said, "These are the ones who were guilty of sins of the flesh."

We moved on to view the next level. There seemed to be something like water poured down on the fire so the flames were smaller—not as intense. Alanus said, "Blood and water from the Side of Jesus continually flows upon the souls on this level." The souls were suffering, but all their suffering seemed more alike, and for some reason, the souls seemed more united. They had their hands raised towards an opening. They seemed to be begging for mercy. Alanus told me, "They suffer intensely for not being in God's Presence."

We moved on to what seemed like a much better area. These souls looked more like people, but they were gray. Alanus said, "These are the ones closest to Paradise. They are almost completely purified. **They need maybe one Mass, or one rosary; maybe one Hail Mary to enter eternal joy**."

"So you see, decorating graves is not what souls, long deceased, cry out for. Many spend long centuries in Purgatory, for their loved ones think they are in Heaven. **If you pray and sacrifice for these Holy Souls, they will assist you now and at the hour of your death.**"

"Make it known."

(May 28, 2007)

REFLECTION ON HOW TO AVOID A LONG STAY IN PURGATORY
By Bishop Ignatius Horstmann
(Bishop of Cleveland, Ohio Diocese 1892-1908)

The Bishop comes. He says: "Praise be to Jesus."

"**Here is the way to avoid a long stay in Purgatory.** Always please God and neighbor ahead of self. The soul that becomes self-absorbed—that is, always considering cost to self in every situation—risks having to spend much more time being purified by the flames of love in Purgatory because of his selfish attitudes."

"Therefore, do not be selfish about the use of your time, money or any spiritual gifts God has given you. Be willing to part with any material goods that are not a necessity. Guide those in Holy Love that God has given you charge over. In humility show gratitude when others do you a favor or compliment you."

"These things I am telling you today are the fulfillment of the Holy Love Message through truth and humility. Remember that anger and impatience, jealousy and avarice, are always signs that you are focusing too much on self. These things should be a signal to you to **refocus on God and others**."

"Pray to the poor souls to help you with this."

(July 25, 2006)

Pray And Sacrifice For The Poor Souls

St. John Vianney: "My brothers and sisters, priests must not be pressured into honoring the dead as already reaching their sainthood. Priests, indeed, have a solemn responsibility to encourage prayer for the faithful departed. Many souls are in Purgatory very close to their release, but no one offers prayer or sacrifice for them. In fact, this is fast becoming a thing of the past."

(April 11, 2008)

PART FOUR

The Battle For Truth

Chapter 19. St. Michael's Shield Of Truth Devotion

****

In This Chapter:

****

"Do not think that when you choose Holy Love over any alternative, that you will not be challenged and set upon by the enemy. Your moment to moment decisions to live in the Divine Will are a frontal attack upon enemy forces. Let your armor be St. Michael's Shield of Truth and your weapon, prayer, which is steeped in Holy Love."

Jesus
Monthly Message to
All People and Every Nation
February 5, 2007

ST. MICHAEL'S SHIELD OF TRUTH PRAYER

*S*t. Michael, you are our defender and safeguard against evil. Place your Shield of Truth over us and defend us in the battle which Satan wages against truth. Help us to see the righteous path of Holy Love.

Clarify our choices between good and evil by placing us always behind your Shield of Truth. Amen.

"I have come to establish in the world a devotion to my Shield which is truth itself. These times are evil. Satan is on the prowl trying to snatch souls from the path of righteousness at every turn. Therefore, Jesus has sent me with this prayer on my lips for all mankind."

St. Michael
March 14, 2006

Promises Attendant to the Prayer

St. Michael: "I have come to state the promises attendant to the prayer of protection behind my Shield of Holy Truth."

"These promises are assured those who with sincere hearts seek the protection of my Shield. But they will be denied those who pray the prayer merely to test its validity."

1. "Those who seek Holy Truth in decisions will be made to see the Light of Truth and the darkness of Satan's lies."

2. "The truths of the Tradition of Faith will be revealed to those who seek this with sincerity. The evil of liberalism will be brought to light."

3. "Satan, who opposes Holy Truth, will not be able to penetrate the Shield I place over hearts. His lies will be repelled by this mighty Shield."

(March 16, 2006)

THE ANOINTING OF ST. MICHAEL

The Blessing may only be extended to one individual at a time. To extend the Blessing, say, think or write:

I extend to *(Insert Name)* the Anointing of St. Michael. Mary, Protectress of the Faith, come to my aid.

St. Michael: "I have come to make known to you that when you extend my blessing—the anointing of St. Michael to a soul—the tip of my Sword pierces the heart of the one you pray for. Thus, in my anointing,

173

the heart is pierced with the truth, for my Sword is also Holy Truth."

(March 19, 2006)

St. Michael: "You ask what about the people who are living a lie in some area of their lives. Our Lady extends this grace to them. Since they believe that the lie or lies they have accepted in their hearts are the truth, they are not open to taking up my Shield."

"But because even the greatest sinner is so loved by the Immaculate Mary, She instructs me to tell you that if you extend the anointing of St. Michael to such a soul, even from a distance, these souls will be given the grace of being shown Holy Truth. Of course, as with any grace, it is up to free will as to whether or not it is accepted."

(March 16, 2006)

Blessed Mother: "...as 'Protectress of the Faith,' I am able to pierce hearts with St. Michael's Sword and hold these hearts open to receive the truth willingly. This way, hearts will not receive the truth one minute and reject it the next."

"Therefore, when you impart to someone the anointing of St. Michael, also say, 'Mary, Protectress of the Faith, come to my aid.' This prayer holds sway over many powers of evil, but not over free will."

(April 29, 2006)

St. Thomas Aquinas: "St. Michael's Shield and his anointing offer the truth, but the soul may, through his

174

free will, choose to reject it. The lies of Satan cannot penetrate the Shield, but the soul with his free will may choose not to accept the truth, but to cling to the lies as he has in the past. St. Michael's Shield is an opportunity of grace. The added petition, 'Mary, Protectress of the Faith, come to my aid,' extends the window of opportunity to accept the truth."

(April 29, 2006)

SHIELD OF TRUTH PRAYER MOVEMENT

Blessed Mother: "Jesus desires in the world the establishment of the Shield of Truth Prayer Movement within the Missionary Servants of Holy Love and the Confraternity itself. This Movement would require:

- one five-decade rosary,
- one United Hearts Chaplet, and
- the St. Michael Shield of Truth Prayer,

daily from each person. This is prescribed so as to form a shield of protection over the entire Mission—protection from Satan's lies."

(June 12, 2006)

Rosary Intention

𝒥 offer this Rosary for those who misunderstand this Mission and the Messages themselves.

175

Chaplet Of The United Hearts

NOTE: *The Chaplet is comprised of twenty (20) beads; five (5) sets each of one (1) Our Father and three (3) Hail Mary's. The following are the meditations of the five (5) sets as given by Our Lady:*

1. In Honor of the Sacred Heart of Jesus

I invite My children to realize the profound depth and perfection that comprises My Beloved Son's Heart. Allow yourselves to be drawn into this Vessel of perfect Love, Mercy, and Truth. Let the Flame of His Heart consume you and bring you to the heights of union with the Holy Trinity. To Him all honor and glory! Jesus, bestow on My children a hunger for salvation through devotion to Your Most Sacred Heart.

(Our Lady / February 7, 1998)
Our Father… Hail Mary… Hail Mary… Hail Mary…

2. In Honor of the Immaculate Heart of Mary

*I*mmaculate Heart of Mary, You are the purest vessel of grace, the definition of holiness, and a sign of the apocalypse. Mary, Your Heart is a Refuge of Holy Love—a countersign in an evil age. Dear Heart of Mary, it has been ordained that the conversion and peace of the world be entrusted to You. Only through Holy Love can the battle be won. As you, Heart of Mary, have been pierced by many swords, impale our hearts with the flaming arrow of Holy Love. Immaculate Heart of Mary, pray for us.

(Our Lady / March 7, 1998)

Our Father… Hail Mary… Hail Mary… Hail Mary…

3. Meditating on the Passion of Our Lord

Jesus was willingly put to death for the sins of mankind. He died for each one and for all. From His side flows, yet today, an unending font of Love and Mercy. Do not be reluctant, as Simon was reluctant, to embrace the crosses you are given. Many suffer the eternal flames of hell, for no one has been willing to suffer for them. Eternal Victim, truly present in the tabernacles of the world, pray for us.

(Our Lady / April 4, 1998)

Our Father… Hail Mary… Hail Mary… Hail Mary…

4. Meditating on the Sorrows of Mary

As My Son suffered for you, I suffered as well, in My intellect, in My heart, and in My body. My physical cross remained hidden. My emotional and intellectual crosses could only be guessed at—the intensity burning within Me. So too, should your suffering remain hidden, whenever possible, to gain merit for souls, grace for the world.

(Our Lady / May 2, 1998)

Our Father… Hail Mary… Hail Mary… Hail Mary…

5. In Atonement to the Hearts of Jesus and Mary

I invite you to understand that your 'yes' in the present moment to Holy Love is atoning to Our United Hearts. I tell you this, My little one, for to live in Holy Love in every moment requires heroic self-discipline and surrender to God's Divine Will through Holy Love. You can sacrifice many great things—possessions, events, and more—but none so great as your own will. This is the greatest atonement.

(Our Lady / June 6, 1998)
Our Father... Hail Mary... Hail Mary... Hail Mary...

(At the end of the Chaplet prayers, on the medal, say the following prayer to the United Hearts of Jesus and Mary.)

Prayer to the United Hearts of Jesus and Mary

O United Hearts of Jesus and Mary, You are all grace, all mercy, all love. Let my heart be joined to Yours, so that my every need is present in Your United Hearts. Most especially, shed Your grace upon this particular need:

> *For those who misunderstand this Mission and the Messages themselves.*

Help me to recognize and accept Your loving will in my life. Amen. Holy and Sacred Wounds of the United Hearts of Jesus and Mary answer my prayer.

ST. MICHAEL'S SHIELD

"I invite you to look closely now at my Shield. Emblazoned upon it are the United Hearts. This is why my Shield is so powerful. The United Hearts are the embodiment of Holy Truth; indeed, the embodiment of the Ten Commandments."

St. Michael
March 16, 2006

Chapter 20. *Protection Of The Faith Prayers*

* *

In This Chapter:

* *

PRAYER FOR PRIESTS

*H*eavenly Mother, I invoke you—take under Your Mantle of Protection all Your priest-sons. Draw them into Your Immaculate Heart—purest vessel of Holy Love. Nurture them in the Tradition of Faith. Give them the grace to reject liberalism. Protect the Church hierarchy from the allurements of liberal theology, power and avarice. Unite them in humility and love, so that the Church will once again be made whole.

Allow the Message of the United Hearts to mend all spiritual illness within the Church. Amen.

"I desire all Confraternity members recite this prayer daily."

Jesus
February 1, 2006

PRAY FOR POPE BENEDICT XVI

Jesus: "This Pontiff is My choice for these troubled times. It is during this Pope's reign much good will be accomplished, and works that were not completed by John Paul II will be completed."

"Do not fear, then, but pray for Pope Benedict as all of Heaven is praying."

(April 26, 2005)

PRAY FOR THE PRIESTHOOD

St. John Vianney: "My brothers and sisters, **pray for all priests that they be spiritually little**, for this way they will not be sophisticated and worldly-wise but will have the singular purpose of saving their flock. Pray that all priests embrace this truth."

(May 13, 2005)

St. John Vianney: "My brothers and sisters, it is of urgent importance that priests be given this message concerning **the path of trustful surrender** which leads to the Divine Will of the Heavenly Father; for it is they who are most under attack, most likely to be pulled from the path by Satan's designs. **Pray that priests accept the path and stay upon it.**"

(January 12, 2007)

St. John Vianney: "My brothers and sisters, **pray that all priests recognize the need to seek the protection of their Heavenly Mother lest they be mislead by liberal theology.** Our Heavenly Mother wants to protect the Faith of all people, but most especially for priests, so that they live and spread only the truths of the Faith."

(November 9, 2007)

Blessed Mother: "My daughter, **today I am asking special prayers and sacrifices for the many priests who are being misled to believe My apparitions here are not genuine.** Through false discernment, Satan has woven his way into the hearts of a few to mislead many. The enemy especially targets priests, for they can touch so many souls."

"It is these few who have opened their hearts to self-righteous error, that have quickly and with certainty, chosen to oppose Heaven and this Mission. If it was you yourself on the path of perdition, if it was you yourself guilty of calumny, detraction and lies, you would want them to pray for you. As it is, they refuse correction, and so, we must pray all the harder for them. I love them, as they are My children, too. **Pray for them, as well as the priests they mislead.**"

(August 20, 2007)

PRAYERS AND GUIDELINES FOR PRIESTS

CONSECRATION TO THE EUCHARISTIC HEART FOR PRIESTS

*M*y Jesus, Divine Good, accept my heart as Your instrument in the world through Holy Love, which is the Immaculate Heart of Mary. I consecrate my vocation in this present moment to Your Eucharistic Heart. I will dedicate my life to bringing the Holy Eucharist to those You lead me to, and to whom I am led.

I desire union and faithfulness to the Will of the Eternal Father through consecration to Your Eucharistic Heart. Amen.

"As there are many priests coming here, both Orthodox and Roman Rite, I desire at this time to address them."

"My brothers, in this present moment, I desire that you rededicate your lives and your vocation. Consecrate yourselves to My Eucharistic Heart through

the Immaculate Heart of My Mother. Then, through the Eucharistic Heart of your Lord and Savior, be consecrated to the Divine Will of the Eternal Father. Through this recommitment, you will live in Divine Love."

Jesus
May 31, 2005

PRAYER TO STRENGTHEN VOCATIONS

$\mathcal{D}$ear Jesus, I place myself under the Complete Blessing of the United Hearts. With this Blessing, I desire a deep understanding of my faults. With your help, I will not defend myself, but by Your assistance, work to overcome every obstacle and weakness that holds me back on the path of holiness.

Impress on my heart a great love for the virtues, most especially Holy Love and Holy Humility, so that every virtue can increase in me. I desire to be holy, and I desire sanctification by living in God's Divine Will. Amen.

"My daughter, I desire that all priests receive and recite this prayer every day from the heart. It will strengthen vocations and boost sagging spirits."

"Priests who faithfully recite this prayer will receive My special protection over their vocations. By My Hand, they will be led to the Heart of the Paternal Father."

Blessed Mother
August 18, 2007

185

Seek Blessed Mother's Protection

St. John Vianney: "Today, my brothers and sisters, vocations are lost and paralyzed because they are not offered to the protection of the Holy Mother. It is She who protects vocations and strengthens them in graces and virtue.

(July 13, 2007)

GUIDELINES FOR PRIESTS

St. John Vianney: "Child of Christ, here are some guidelines for priests—not only the ones who come here, but also the ones who are deciding about the Messages or the Confraternity."

1. "Frequent confession after much soul-searching."

2. "Pray for discernment. An opinion or a judgment is not discernment. Realize that today some Dioceses are compromised by error—by liberalism."

3. "Use your guardian angel. Develop a love for this angel God has given you."

4. "Love the souls in your charge, and do all in your power to bring them to salvation."

5. "Be humble and childlike. Avoid intellectual pride. Give all credit to God from your heart."

6. "Pray for the Poor Souls. They have much power. Put them to use."

"If priests follow these guidelines, Jesus promises a strengthening of their vocations."

(November 1, 2007)

FOR THE REMNANT FAITHFUL

SEARCH FOR TRUTH ACCORDING TO THE TRADITION OF FAITH

Father, Son and Holy Spirit, grant me—

Temperance—not to accept everything at face value.
Prudence—to search out the truth.
Wisdom—to recognize the truth. Amen"

"The Remnant will always recognize the truth when it is based upon Holy and Divine Love…"
"I will help you. I am your strength. I will not abandon you, if you believe."

Jesus' April 5, 2008 Monthly Message to
All People and Every Nation

PRAYER ON BEHALF OF
THE REMNANT FAITHFUL

*E*ternal Father, take the Remnant Church which You have formed, into Your Paternal Heart. Protect the Deposit of Faith from the arrows of compromise and deceit. Your Heart, dear Father, is the Flame of Righteousness and Truth. Keep the Remnant Faithful secure in this Eternal Flame. Amen.

"Special grace will be given to those who pray this prayer with a sincere heart so that they will readily recognize compromise."

Jesus
February 5, 2007

Pray That Your Numbers Increase

Jesus: "As children of the light, I invoke you, pray that your numbers increase. In this way, the Remnant Faithful will be strengthened."
(June 5, 2007 / Monthly Message
to All People and Every Nation)

*Chapter 21. Prayers
For The Mission*

✱✱✱

In This Chapter:

✱✱✱

PRAYER TO THE PRECIOUS BLOOD

Sweet Precious Blood of Jesus, pour out upon this Mission and the Confraternity. Set us free from anything that may distract our journey into the United Hearts. Immerse us in Divine Love—Divine Mercy. Amen.

Jesus
February 17, 2004

PRAYER TO PROPAGATE THE SPIRITUALITY OF THE CHAMBERS OF THE UNITED HEARTS

*D*ear Blessed Mother, through the grace of Your Immaculate Heart, give me the courage to propagate the spirituality of the Chambers of the United Hearts through the spreading of these Messages. Help me to be Your instrument in the face of opposition so that this spirituality is perpetuated in generations to come. Amen.

Jesus
September 8, 2007

Pray To Set Souls On Fire

Jesus: "When you pray, pray that souls are set on fire with a zeal for evangelizing the Chambers of Our United Hearts. I desire that those who choose this path—this spiritual journey—be united in making the Message known. We must work together, realizing the importance of one soul at a time. Realize, as well, that each one's spiritual journey is one step at a time."

(December 15, 2005)

THE CHAMBERS OF THE UNITED HEARTS OF THE HOLY TRINITY AND IMMACULATE MARY

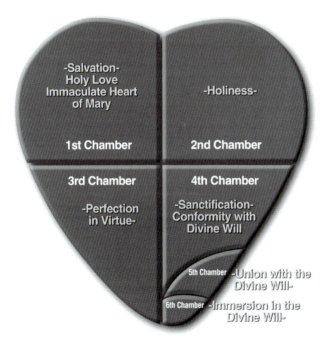

The Door to Each Chamber is Deeper Surrender to Love – the Divine Will

PROPAGATE THE MESSAGES

Jesus: "Whenever you ask for Heavenly assistance in propagating this Message of Our United Hearts, you will receive it, even in the most unlikely circumstances. Never be afraid, then, to be My Hands, My Feet, My Voice amongst unbelievers. Witness to the world the power of Holy Love. Draw people to Me by your example. I will abundantly bless you."

(April 14, 2006)

Jesus: "Today I remind you—not to choose to be part of My Army of Love—is to choose. You must be with Me. There is a battle going on in hearts—a spiritual battle— between good and evil that most do not recognize. I am appointing each of you who live according to these Messages to be recruitment officers for this Army of Love, by spreading the Messages, by praying the Rosary of the Unborn; for this, too, is a way of bringing souls to Me."

(July 5, 2007 / Monthly Message to
All People and Every Nation)

PRAY FOR THOSE WHO OPPOSE THE MISSION

Jesus: "Understand, My messenger, that when free will rationalizes against the Messages here, it opens the heart to the father of lies. This rationalization is the self-righteous error I have spoken to you about.

Such rationalization does not hold itself accountable, is not convicted and, therefore, unrepentant. Such a one has fallen into Satan's grasp and has become his instrument."

"**Continue to pray for those who have set themselves at odds with this Mission.** Here, Heaven has touched earth. The inner Chambers of My Heart have been revealed to all. The call has been sent forth for conversion of all mankind through Holy and Divine Love."

(August 29, 2007)

Jesus: "…you must pray for those who oppose this Ministry, for this is the loving thing to do. Your prayers for your enemies bind Satan's hands and keep him from fulfilling his plans of destruction."

(May 27, 2005)

Jesus: "My dear brothers and sisters, when you pray for your enemies and all those who oppose you in the world, **pray that they are scattered in the conceit of their hearts**. This way they will lose their focus of evil and their direction of opposition against you. Then My Mother's grace will be able to conquer their hearts."

(June 8, 2003)

PRAYER OF INTERCESSION TO GOD THE FATHER FOR HOLY LOVE MINISTRIES *BASED ON JUDITH 9: 5 – 19* *(Douay-Rheims)*
Composed by a Priest

O, my Eternal Father, please hear me. You are the Eternal Now, the Author of all time, space and events – all things visible and invisible. You created every present moment, and the future You have planned. As Father of all creation, whatever You devise comes into being; the things You decide upon come forward as we consecrate every present moment to Holy and Divine Love, which is Your Divine Will.

All Your Ways are according to Your Ordaining Will and Your Judgment is Your Permitting Will made with foreknowledge.

My Eternal Father, here before Your Remnant Faithful is a vast force, filled with pride and boasting of their power in self-love; trusting only in themselves. They do not know that You, The Eternal Now, crush self-love with Holy Love, Your Divine Will.

Shatter their strength of inordinate self-love and crush their force of false beliefs and lies with St. Michael's Shield of Truth, for they have resolved to profane all that You have created in some way; be it through evil or self-will, and to compromise the Church where the True Presence of Your Son resides so as to overthrow Your Sovereignty by serving the god of self-love.

See their pride and, through the Heart of the Immaculate Mary, send forth the Flame of Holy Love to illuminate hearts and annihilate the error of their self-will.

And strengthen me Heavenly Father in Holy and Divine Love. With my prayer, reveal the areas of pride in my life and crush the strength of their pride with Your Hands of Holy and Divine Humility which reside in the United Hearts of Jesus and Mary.

Your strength, O Lord, is <u>not</u> in numbers, nor does Your power depend upon stalwart men; but You are the God of the lowly, the Helper of the oppressed, the Supporter of the weak, the Protector of the forsaken Remnant Faithful in the tradition of Faith. Please, please, Eternal Father, Lord of Heaven and Earth, Creator and King of the Universe, hear my prayer that error in pride-filled hearts is corrected and harmony restored between Your Divine Will and men's free will. Bring confusion on those who have planned dire things against Your Divine Will; Your Covenant of Love, Your Holy Temple – the Church, and the homes Your little children have inherited. Let all peoples and every nation know clearly that You are the God of all power and might Who directs all things in love and that there is no other one who protects us but You alone.

For I believe that in Your Infinite Wisdom You know better than I what is good for humanity. I believe that in Your Infinite Power You can bring good even out of evil. I believe that in Your Infinite Goodness You bring everything to the advantage of those who love You above all else; so that even under the hands of those who strike me – I kiss Your Hands of Holy and Divine Love which heal.

Teach me to always see Your Love as my guide in every event of my life. Teach me to surrender myself to You like a baby in its mother's arms. Help me to consecrate every present moment to Holy and Divine Love, for I understand it is only through Holy and Divine Love that mankind can be reconciled with his Creator. Amen.

SHIELD OF TRUTH PRAYER MOVEMENT

(Please see Chapter 19)

Blessed Mother: "Jesus desires in the world the establishment of the Shield of Truth Prayer Movement within the Missionary Servants of Holy Love and the Confraternity itself… so as to form a shield of protection over the entire Mission—protection from Satan's lies."

(June 12, 2006)

Chapter 22. *Prayer Chambers*

****

In This Chapter:

Format for Individuals
Format for Groups

****

"I am your Jesus, born Incarnate."

"I have come to encourage the formation of prayer cells* within individual hearts and within groups wherever possible. None has the excuse of too little time to form a prayer cell within his own heart. There are 24 hours within a day. A prayer cell—recitation of five-decade rosary, the United Hearts chaplet and meditation on a message—takes perhaps 30 minutes."

January 31, 2005

*NOTE: "Prayer Cells" and "Prayer Chambers" are one and the same.

197

BASIC FORMAT FOR INDIVIDUALS

1. United Hearts Chaplet

2. One 5-decade rosary

3. Meditation on a Holy and Divine Love message

> Jesus: "Stay close to Me. **Make your heart into a little prayer chamber where you can retreat**; then the Holy Spirit will come and tell you what you need to know.
>
> (February 27, 2005)

BASIC FORMAT FOR GROUPS

1. United Hearts Chaplet

2. One 5-decade Rosary *(any of the sets of Rosary meditations are appropriate)*

3. Consecration to the Flame of Holy Love

4. Reading of a message on Holy and Divine Love, with possible instruction on it, if a priest is available

5. Review of a Lesson on the Virtues *(from tapes or booklets available through Archangel Gabriel Enterprises Inc.)*

Possible Enhancements to the Format

1. **Fifteen decades of the Rosary** rather than five.

    Use of various Rosary meditations includes any of the sets of Rosary meditations given to the Missionary Servants of Holy Love. (See the *Triumphant Hearts Prayer Book* and the *United Hearts Book of Prayers and Meditations.*)

2. **Use of other prayers** as desired from the *Triumphant Hearts Prayer Book* and the *United Hearts Book of Prayers and Meditations* are also encouraged.

NOTE: *The leaders may use their discernment as to the general level, and therefore source of study, for the particular group as described below.*

---

3. **If the emphasis of a particular meeting is the Missionary Servants of Holy Love Secular Order** (working on the spirituality of the First Chamber of Jesus' Heart—salvation), reflection on one of the Scripture selections or journal entries in volume

199

one of the *Triumphant Hearts Prayer Book* may be advisable, in addition to the regular format described herein. The Chapters on Holy Love from *Heaven's Last Call to Humanity*, and from *Holy and Divine Love: The Remedy and the Triumph* are also highly recommended.

4. **If the emphasis of the particular meeting is the Confraternity of the United Hearts** (working on the spirituality of the deeper Chambers of Jesus' Heart—holiness, perfection, and union), then the prayers of *Consecration to Divine Love* are particularly appropriate additions to the regular format described herein. The compilations available on the Divine Love messages and the Chambers of the Sacred Heart of Jesus are also highly recommended.

5. **Study on the virtues** for any Prayer Chamber meeting can be augmented by the compilation of Virtue messages available from Archangel Gabriel Enterprises Inc.

6. **Blessings of the United Hearts, of Holy Love, and of Divine Love** may be extended to all present, with emphasis on the Divine Source and effects of the Blessings, rather than an extravagant ceremony of extension by any particular individual.

Chapter 23. *Confraternity Prayers*

* *

In This Chapter:

* *

GUIDELINES FOR THE CONFRATERNITY

Jesus: "Those who would consider joining the Confraternity should accomplish the following daily:"

1. "Pursue the spiritual journey through the Chambers of Our United Hearts."

2. "Recite the Confraternity Rosary daily."

3. "Recite the Chaplet of the United Hearts for living and deceased members of the Confraternity."

4. "Perform corporal and/or spiritual works of mercy. One of the spiritual works can be propagation of the Confraternity itself."

5. "Pray for priests."

6. "Daily consecration to Divine Love and Our United Hearts."

(March 17, 2003)

DAILY PRAYER INTENTIONS

Jesus: "Today, I request that each member of the Confraternity offer:

1. "A prayer daily for the propagation of the Confraternity, both in hearts and in the world."

2. "A prayer daily for the unification of the Universal Church in the Tradition of Faith."

3. "A prayer daily for personal holiness."

4. "A prayer daily for those who receive the message of the Chambers of the United Hearts, but reject it out of pride."

5.   "A prayer daily that all will live in the Divine Will."

"These prayers can be nothing more than the ejaculation—'**Jesus, Triumph and Reign**'—or they can be a decade of the rosary for each intention. The latter would be known as '**The Rosary of the Confraternity**'."

(February 7, 2003)

THE ROSARY OF THE CONFRATERNITY OF THE UNITED HEARTS

Jesus: "This is how I desire the Rosary of the Confraternity be prayed. Before each meditation on each mystery of the rosary, the intention is given with the following supplications."

1.   "We pray this decade for the propagation of the Confraternity, both in hearts and in the world. We understand that the Confraternity will usher in the Victory of the United Hearts."

2.   "We offer this decade for the unification of the Universal Church in the Tradition of Faith. We pray that what is in darkness will be brought into the light, and compromise will face defeat."

3. "*We offer* this decade for our own personal holiness. We pray to be perfected in Holy Love— thereby being led deep into Divine Love."

4. "*We pray* this decade for all who receive the Message of the Chambers of the United Hearts, but reject it out of pride. We ask the Blessed Mother to give them the grace of the illumination of conscience."

5. "*We offer* this decade that all will live in the Divine Will. The Kingdom to come is the reign of the Divine Will in every heart. This is the Triumph and Victory."
    (February 8, 2003)

UNITED HEARTS CHAPLET

Jesus: "The Confraternity carries to its membership not only the call to salvation, but an even deeper call to sanctification and union with the Divine Will."

"Therefore, I am extending this grace to all its members—that the recitation of the United Hearts Chaplet be recited daily by each member of this Confraternity for the spiritual well-being of all the membership."

(February 7, 2003)

PRAYER FOR PRIESTS

*H*eavenly Mother, I invoke you—take under Your Mantle of Protection all Your priest sons. Draw them into Your Immaculate Heart—purest vessel of Holy Love.

Nurture them in the Tradition of Faith. Give them the grace to reject liberalism. Protect the Church hierarchy from the allurements of liberal theology, power and avarice. Unite them in humility and love, so that the Church will once again be made whole.

Allow the Message of the United Hearts to mend all spiritual illness within the Church. Amen.

"I desire all Confraternity members recite this prayer daily."

Jesus
February 1, 2006

PRAYER TO THE PRECIOUS BLOOD

*S*weet Precious Blood of Jesus, pour out upon this Mission and the Confraternity. Set us free from anything that may distract our journey into the United Hearts. Immerse us in Divine Love—Divine Mercy. Amen.

"Pray this daily."

Jesus
February 17, 2004

PRAYER TO THE HOLY SOULS IN PURGATORY ON BEHALF OF THE CONFRATERNITY

*D*ear Holy Souls, I have confidence in your power to bring petitions before the Throne of God. During this present moment, hear my petition for the protection and propagation of the Confraternity of the United Hearts.

You understand the great need for this spiritual journey through the Will of God. Therefore, I feel confident in your intercession.

"The Holy Souls in Purgatory are able to unite in prayer for certain causes. Their petitions are efficaciously heard by the United Hearts."

"Today I desire you take this prayer to the world on behalf of the Confraternity."

Jesus
May 31, 2007

SHIELD OF TRUTH PRAYER MOVEMENT

(Please see Chapter 19)

Blessed Mother: "Jesus desires in the world the establishment of the Shield of Truth Prayer Movement within the Missionary Servants of Holy Love and the Confraternity itself… so as to form a shield of protection over the entire Mission—protection from Satan's lies."

(June 12, 2006)

REFLECTIONS ON HEAVEN'S CALL

"I am your Jesus, born Incarnate."

"The Confraternity, simply put, is My call to Catholics to live out this spiritual journey in holiness. Within the Confraternity, souls will be spiritually nourished through teachings, and gain strength for the journey through the sacraments. This is not to say I exclude non-Catholics from making the journey, for I call all people, all nations into the Chambers of My Heart."

"I call attention, in particular, to this universal call by sounding the trumpet blast universally into the First Chamber. Do not be mistaken—the First Chamber cannot be bypassed. It is the basis and foundation of all the others. No one progresses spiritually without first being purified in the Flame of My Mother's Heart. Who amongst you can become more holy without knowing himself better?"

(August 12, 2007)

"I am your Jesus, born Incarnate."

"My child, please understand that My goal is to win souls over to this spiritual journey. It does not concern Me what label, or if any label, is placed upon peoples' response to the call to personal holiness. The arguments in the world today against My call, center on labels—is it approved—is it ecumenical?"

"I am calling everyone, and excluding no one, from the journey through Our Hearts. I offer the Confraternity as a vehicle to this end, for the sacraments strengthen and assist the soul in the journey. Do not squabble amongst yourselves as to how to make the journey, or as to who can make the journey. Only follow Me!"

(August 12, 2007)

Chapter 24.  **Pilgrim Prayers**

* *

In This Chapter:

Pilgrimage Preparation
Prayer to be Recited by Pilgrims Visiting
     Maranatha Spring and Shrine
Prayer for Healing with Maranatha Water
Maranatha Graces and Blessings
Instructions to Pilgrims

* *

PILGRIMAGE PREPARATION

"I am your Jesus, born Incarnate. It is important for the pilgrims to know that their journey here [Maranatha Spring and Shrine] is a pilgrimage, not a holiday. As such, they should **prepare in advance with prayer and sacrifice** so that their hearts are ready to receive the graces that are offered here."

"When they enter the property, they are offered the embrace of Our United Hearts. If their hearts are properly disposed, the embrace will prepare them for an illumination of conscience, as St. Michael's sword pricks their heart."

209

"I desire that each pilgrim returns the embrace to Our United Hearts by living the Message of Holy and Divine Love in their own hearts. This, in itself, is all the recompense I ask."

"With a heart full of love, accept any inconvenience that this journey presents. I speak not only of the journey here to this site, but the journey through the Chambers of Our United Hearts, as well."

"You will please make this known."

(March 27, 2006)

PRAYER TO BE RECITED BY PILGRIMS VISITING MARANATHA SPRING AND SHRINE

Dear Heavenly Mother, I know you have called me to this place of Your favor for Your purpose. As I step onto the property You have chosen as Your own, help me to realize that You are inviting me into a deeper personal conversion through the Revelation of the United Hearts. Help me to begin this journey by stepping into Your Heart which is Holy Love.

If You, Blessed Mother, look into my heart and see that I am unprepared or unwilling to take this first step, extend Your Hand filled with grace towards me and I will take it.

Do not allow me, Your child, to pass up this opportunity through doubts or pride. If I came here only looking for error, take this spirit of arrogance away, dear Mother.

I desire to be Yours in this present moment through Holy Love. Amen.

"Here, child, is a prayer I desire all who journey in pilgrimage to the prayer site, recite."

Jesus
May 22, 2004

PRAYER FOR HEALING WITH MARANATHA WATER
(While making the Sign of the Cross)

*D*ear Jesus, as I bless myself with this water, open my heart to the grace Heaven desires I have. Let me look into my soul with the eyes of truth. Give me the courage and humility to do so. Heal me according to the Will of Your Father. Amen.

"I desire that this little prayer be recited whenever any water from this property be used in making the Sign of the Cross."

"It is not necessary that the water be blessed prior to its use in this way by a priest. Heaven releases many graces at this Site [Maranatha Spring and Shrine] and with this water."

(Later that day)

"My brothers and sisters, do not be surprised that in the healing prayer I imparted to the world this

morning, I placed **healing of the heart and soul** *first and foremost; for this is the main purpose of this Mission—the conversion of souls.* **Those who come here should open themselves to this grace** *so that I can work in them and bring them closer to Me."*

Jesus
January 18, 2008

MARANATHA GRACES AND BLESSINGS

Jesus: "My brothers and sisters, I invite you to understand that the greatest grace, the greatest miracle given at this site is the grace to live in Holy Love in the present moment. Appreciate this; ask for it when you come here and it will be granted. You are given special angels to assist you."

(September 5, 2005 / Monthly Message
to All Nations)

Jesus: "Grace abounds here. The message is the only message he need hear, because it envelops every message. At the property or through the use of the water at the many sources there present, the pilgrim will receive the illumination of conscience. He may be physically healed or receive the grace to carry his cross."

(May 3, 2001)

St. Pio of Pietrelcina: "There is no one who comes here that leaves without some type of healing—physical, spiritual or emotional. If they have a physical cross, it is either removed at the Spring, or they receive the grace to bear the cross of their affliction more admirably. This, in itself, is a healing. If the cross comes as an emotional affliction, the same is true. The cross is either removed or lightened."

"Therefore, let no one say, 'I came, but was not healed.' The same is true wherever Heaven meets earth—Lourdes, Fatima—all the great places of pilgrimage."

(September 30, 2006)

Jesus: "Those who come to the property experience this Blessing [of Paternal Love] if their hearts are open, and if they accept the Messages of Holy and Divine Love. It gives peace."

(July 24, 2007)

Jesus: "When I extend to you My Blessing of Divine Love as I often do at this site, it extends over you and in you abundant grace to choose the Divine Will in every present moment."

(April 7, 2001)

Jesus: "Know that everyone who comes onto the property receives My Anointing of Divine Love. It is up to each individual to receive or reject what I give here."

(March 3, 2008)

INSTRUCTIONS TO PILGRIMS

St. Catherine of Siena says: "Praise be to Jesus."

"I wish to describe to you the proper disposition of heart for those who come to this apparition site—especially for the first time. Jesus desires that the heart of each pilgrim be open—that the heart be a blank page for Him to write upon. The less the pilgrim knows of others' opinions, the better. There are, as with every apparition site, many false rumors and false discernment attacking this place of Heaven's predilection."

"Jesus does not like people to come with preconceived ideas of what may take place here. Therefore, do not anticipate any certain grace. Each one's pilgrimage is individual. Some may receive a profound illumination of conscience—others not."

"Do not look for proof of all that takes place here as being from Heaven. Do not come here to find fault. That is not discernment."

"Let your hearts be open to the individual experience that God has in store for you, knowing full well that Immaculate Mary invited you here to deepen your relationship with Her Son and God the Father. Allow the Spirit of Truth to carry you deeper into an intimate relationship with the Holy Trinity."

"Do not compare your experience here with anyone else's, for no two are alike. God knows best how to reach each heart. When you share your experiences, do so giving God the glory, for all grace comes from His Mercy and His Love. Never present yourself as being chosen or special or all-knowing in any way. Remember, humility is the first step on the stairway to holiness. There is a proper way to evangelize just as there is a proper way to do anything."

"Do not allow your heart to be filled with judgment against Heaven's efforts here. You do not gain merit in God's Eyes by opposing Him. You only invoke His Judgment. Such a one cooperates with evil."

"Make a sincere heartfelt Act of Contrition before you come onto the property. Grace will then fill your heart."

(April 24, 2008)

Messages Of Truth

I see a great Flame that I understand represents the Heart of God the Father. I hear a voice say: "I am the Eternal Now—Creator of Heaven and earth."

"…I have sent My Son into the world to give you life-yielding Messages of truth here on this Site. You now know the direct path to My Paternal Heart, to the Light of the Spirit, the Divine Heart of Jesus and the Immaculate Heart of the Virgin Mary. All of these come gift wrapped to you in My Divine Will. Herein is the path of salvation, holiness, sanctification and world peace. Are you listening?"

INDEX

INDEX

****

INDEX

****

INDEX

INDEX

INDEX

****

Additional Resources Available Through Archangel Gabriel Enterprises Inc.

(Please visit the Holy Love website for downloadable books and images.)

Books and Booklets

The Chambers of the Divine, Sacred Heart of Jesus
Confraternity of the United Hearts Member Handbook
Confraternity of the United Hearts Prayer Life
Conversations with Divine Love
Devotion to the Mournful Heart of Jesus
Discernment: Discovering the Truth
Divine Love
First Chamber of the United Hearts—Holy Love
Heaven Speaks to the Heart of the World
Heaven's Last Call to Humanity
Holy and Divine Love Messages for Priests
Holy and Divine Love Messages on the Eucharist
Holy and Divine Love: The Remedy and the Triumph
Lessons on the Virtues
Message of Christ's Mystical Church of Atonement
Messages from God the Father
Messages from Heaven on Faith, Hope, Love and
  Trust
Messages from St. John Vianney
Messages from St. Peter on Temptation
Messages from St. Rita on Perseverance
Messages from St. Thomas Aquinas
Our Lady Gives the World the Rosary of the Unborn
Our Lady's Messages at the Arbor

Pilgrim Photos: Through the Eye of the Camera
Pilgrim's Guide to Maranatha Spring and Shrine
Purgatory
The Revelation of Our United Hearts: The Secrets
  Revealed
St. Michael's Shield of Truth Devotion
Triumphant Hearts Prayer Book
Truth
United Hearts Book of Prayers and Meditations
Visions of Saints

Devotional Items

Chaplet of the Unborn
Chaplet of the United Hearts
Divine Victimhood Pin
Maranatha Spring Water Bottle
Mary, Protectress of the Faith Medal
Mournful Heart of Jesus Medal
Rosary of the Unborn *(5-decade or 1-decade)*
United Hearts Scapular *(Cloth or Medal)*

Published by:
Archangel Gabriel Enterprises Inc.
37137 Butternut Ridge Rd.
North Ridgeville, OH 44039   USA
Phone: 440-327-4532
E-Mail: customerservice@RosaryoftheUnborn.com
To order online: http://www.RosaryoftheUnborn.com
ISBN: 978-1-937800-37-6
Holy Love Website: http://www.holylove.org